Where Did *That* Come From?

I Never Thought Of It That Way

Where Did *That* Come From?

I Never Thought Of It That Way

Victoria Thomas Poller

Table of Content

Acknowledgements.. 7
A Poem.. 78
A Secret Place.. 121
A Wife... 20
About The Author.. 156
Ain't Too Proud.. 91
Allegiance.. 118
Are You a Player or a Spectator?.............................. 76
Are Your Antennas Up For God's Call?..................... 152
Ask and Receive.. 102
Asking and Receiving.. 103
Bad Habits... 92
Be Positive... 47
Being Critical... 45
Being Humble, Not Humiliated................................... 135
Being Kind in All Things... 71
Believe and Receive.. 141
Boy, I'm Lucky.. 17
Busy, Busy, Busy... 34
Called By God Or Man?.. 85
Can I Borrow...?.. 143
Care About Someone... 107
Check in Your Spirit.. 68
Choirs and Commitment... 41
Chow Time.. 120
Christianity... 61
Christian Woman!.. 113
Communion... 39
Consider Your Ways... 63
Creating A Blessing... 70
Dancing Machine.. 38
Deceptive Production.. 90
Didn't You See Me?... 22
Do Not Disturb!!!... 92
Don't Be Hard Hearted.. 32
Don't Wanna Go.. 139
Do You Believe?.. 63
Does the Church Have a Head Cold?.......................... 22
Double Time.. 69
Dress... 95
Dueling Paper Mates.. 137
Eat, Drink and Be Merry.. 128
Entertaining Angels... 62
Fear vs. Faith... 138
First Things First... 152
Fixed Income... 116
Forgiven.. 42
Getting Even.. 90
Give It Up - Turn It Loose – Let It Alone!................... 82
God Bless You... 15
God Does Not Argue... 47
God Our Parent.. 44

Table of Content

God Parenting... 150
God's Got a Super Highway.. 130
God Told Me To, Didn't He?.. 106
Good Girls.. 94
Heard It Through the Grapevine.. 124
Hearing God... 79
Hearing God Pt 2.. 151
Hearsay.. 35
Hear – Understand – Do... 30
Heaven... 48
Heavenly Brownie Points.. 140
Help!.. 66
Help Wanted... 35
He's Always On Call... 53
Hey Mon, You Got The Time?... 97
Hold On – Be Strong.. 72
Home Alone.. 45
"Homo vs. Hetero?"- No Question....................................... 115
Horror Stories.. 24
Humility.. 38
I Acknowledge You.. 10
I Serve a Big God.. 113
I Want To Have.. 65
I Don't Wanna Lord... 129
I'm Only Kidding.. 99
Incest... 98
Interpretation... 15
It's All Right, Not!.. 90
It's In There... 91
Jonah's Prayer 2: 2-10 (Modern Interpretation)......................... 55
"Joy" Fruit of the Spirit.. 125
Just Do It!.. 94
Know Who You're Calling... 92
Lenten and New Years Resolutions... 147
Let's Give Jesus A Hand.. 124
License.. 98
Life is Not a Soap Opera... 78
Lifting Holy Hands... 25
Listen My Children.. 151
Listen To What You Hear... 136
Live and Let Live.. 138
Lookin' Them Straight In the Eye.. 149
Looking For Love... 61
Making the Difference... 123
Man.. 74
Manifestations.. 83
Me And Mine.. 68
Milk vs. Meat... 60
Miracle Manifestation.. 84
More About Sin... 115
More On Praise and Worship... 41

Table of Content

More on Rescue 911 82
Motivation 122
Music 17
Never Let Them See You Sweat 16
No Clue 31
No Fear 128
Now I Really Know Him 144
Open Your Eyes 64
Open Sez-A-Me 130
Operator 52
Order 73
Our Children Have To Leave Sometimes 43
Patience 112
Paying Prayer to the Holy Spirit 14
Pennies From Heaven 37
Perfect 111
Perfect Forty 145
Picture (Choir) 40
Picture (Dueling Paper Mates) 137
Picture (Move The Mountain) 102
Picture (Telephone) 52
Picture This 86
Praise/Worship 40
Praising God or Praising god? 142
Prayer 53
Preface 8
Psalm 68:11 155
Question 69
Quit Skating And Start Working 87
Raise Your Hands If You're Sure 27
Reach Out and Touch 149
Reading the Bible 14
Regarding Love 95
Rescue 911 81
Right Here and Now 99
Santa Clause 73
Saved or Being Judgmental? 35
Scrumdidileyumschious! 120
Seeking the Right Thing 112
Shout 15
Shower Full-O-Blessings 139
Sin, Suicide and Such 93
Sincere, Or Not Sincere 49
Somebody's Watching You 123
Some of Those Who Walked Before God 18
Sore Tootsies 130
Sorry Lord 110
Speak 34
Speak To Me Lord 81
Spirits vs. Spirits 113
Spiritual Boxing Gloves 146
Stay Home and Rest Awhile 109

Table of Content

Stealing.. 119
Superstition.. 116
Taking Advantage.. 127
Tell Somebody.. 106
Temptation.. 77
Thank You...For What?.. 49
The Anointing – Falling Under the Power – Time Out........................ 56
The Apostles Creed.. 96
The Bible.. 13
The Cigarette Situation.. 67
The Church Is a Business.. 153
The Gift.. 94
The Gifts of the Spirit – Promises of God.. 28
The Lord's Prayer.. 89
The Monument.. 72
The Tongue.. 33
The World Didn't Give It,.. 120
This Is Not My Home.. 100
Tithes.. 117
To Be, Or Not Too Be - Selfish.. 104
To Have and To Hold.. 42
To View or Not to View.. 79
Tried And True.. 76
Truths to Our Beliefs.. 69
Ushers.. 88
Virtual Reality.. 23
Waste Not – Want Not.. 51
Watch Rationale.. 66
We Have To Realize God.. 136
Welfare.. 126
We Must Work, While It Is Day.. 43
"We" vs. "I".. 46
"We" vs. "I" (Part II).. 46
What Have You Done To Be Tired?.. 51
What is a Prophet?.. 62
What Is A Testimony?.. 47
What's A Blessing?.. 16
What's On Sale?.. 36
Where's the Faith?.. 12
Where's The Rock?.. 89
Who Are You Trying To Convince?.. 96
Who Do You Trust?.. 85
Who or What Are You a Slave To?.. 132
Who's On First?.. 131
Who's The Captain Of Your Team?.. 66
Why Do Christians Gather Together?.. 80
Wise Men.. 97
Wishing and Waiting.. 87
Wow!.. 92
Xmas.. 122
You've Got To Earn It.. 106

Acknowledgments

"In all thy ways acknowledge Him, and He shall direct thy paths." Proverbs 3:6

Allow me to give almighty God all the praise, glory & honor. He is my creator. It is through the blessings of my Lord, that I was given the ability to write the contents of this book.

Through Christ, I have been blessed with an understanding and a supporting family (my husband Levan, my son Robert, and my daughter Tonya).

I would also like to give thanks to all those who have encouraged me, and to those persons present, and to those who have gone on to be with the Lord, who gave spiritual counsel through words and/or deeds.

Through constant communication with the Holy Spirit, I finally realized that it was time to put this endeavor into action.

Special thanks to JR Jones for all her professional input and suggestions.

And last, but not least – Thank you, dear reader, for your support. I hope that you will be blessed with the turn of every page.

All biblical references are from the King James Version (KJV), Modern King James Version (MKJV), Living Bible (LB), and Good News Bible (GN). Any reference to God the Father, Son, or Holy Spirit, the Bible or His Holy Word, will appear in capital letters.

Definitions are from: http://dictionary.reference.com/ unless otherwise specified.

Cover & "Move the Mountain" Illustration By:

Robert L. Poller

Consultation and Layout By:

Levan R. Poller

Preface

"Where Did That Come From? I Never Thought of It That Way" is a non-fiction book that some people describe as a narrative collection of "disjointed thoughts." One piece may not have anything to do with the previous story or the next account of events, but it contains anecdotes that will make you say to yourself, "She's talking about me again." You, the reader, can either say, "Ouch" or "Amen." I know that I have said either one or the other myself.

It is *not* a novel that sticks to one subject, but it is a variety of thought-provoking topics and nuggets of information such as rituals that occur in church that you may not understand, how to act in public, what to do when you don't want to hold your peace, how to treat other people, how to approach the ten commandments, getting in touch with yourself, getting close to God, and much more. There may be some things, which you've heard before, and there may be some new revelations that make you say, "Hmmm?"

This author's aim is not to take away from, nor add to the Word of God; but to offer *hope*. All of the excerpts in this book are to encourage the reader to think about *it*. This book is not judgmental but is intended to help the reader to take a look at him- or her self and those who may have an influence upon the reader's life. This author's main goal is to win souls for Jesus. If some have planted and some have watered, then it is my intent to have God to give the increase.

Some of the short stories have been confirmed through other ministers of God's Word. Ministers of good news will say something that will spark the unction of the Holy Spirit in me to write on that particular subject. I continue to listen to the Holy Spirit while I'm in my quiet place (usually the bathroom, kitchen, or just being still), and I take notes—a lot of notes. I keep a pen and notepad at my bedside, in the car, and in my purse because I want to be ready when I need to take dictation from the Holy One.

I am a teacher of God's Word. The messages from God, through this minister, may *not* make you shout or clap your hands but usually the words are things that will help you to consider your ways and the path in which you may choose to go. Happy Reading!

I Acknowledge You

Do you know how sometimes you feel that God is not listening? Or you've checked everything that you know according to the ordinances of God's will, and it seems that your prayers are not reaching Gods' ear? It happens to the best of us. Yet, rest assured that God hears, He understands, and He is working on your situation.

He lets us know that He hears us. He tells us, in a subtle small way, that only God could make happen, that all is well and for us to hold out until later.

For example: one day while walking my dog, I was also talking with a friend, and she inquired if I ever had a problem with my refrigerator in my fifth-wheel. It's not usual for recreational vehicle (RV) refrigerators to need defrosting every week, but hers did. I told her about a repairman that we had service our refrigerator about six months earlier. Mind you—I now reside in a city where you can go weeks and weeks without seeing a particular person, or have them pop up. As I was finishing the walk with my dog, Pugsley, I met the RV repairman coming up the path towards me. I hadn't seen him or his truck in over six months, yet there he was. I asked him to stop by my friend's and see about her RV.

You may *not* think that was something special, but I believe it to be God letting me know that He heard everything. Some things may happen right away, as that incident did, and other expectations may take longer.

When things take longer than we anticipate, it's usually because what we request from God is not His *best* for us at that time. It may not be arriving on *our* so-called timetable, but, if we wait and allow God to be God, then we will receive the abundant, bountiful blessings of The Most High. *"And let us not be weary in well doing: for in due season we shall reap, if we faint not" (Gal. 6:9).*

Consider the story of Joseph.[1] Here was a man favored by his daddy. Jealous brothers sold him (instead of killing him), into slavery in a foreign country, because he was "All that and a bag of chips." The Brother had game. (a gift).

Although a slave in his new place, Joseph was shown favor in the household of his new master. Sometimes we too are blessed, and we think it's the greatest blessing that God would have for us—but it's *not* God's best.

Misfortune again came upon Joseph when his master's wife seduced him. She then lied on him, and he was thrown into prison. Yet, God let Joseph know that he was not alone and God was still abiding with him. Joseph became the head-dog-in-charge of the prison and the other inmates. Again, Joseph was tested (sounds like our lives, doesn't it?). He was asked to be a *dream interpreter*.

The man was so good at what he did that the Pharaoh of Egypt called for him. How about that? Joseph went "*From the Pit to the Palace.*" In the end, Joseph's brothers had to become

---

[1] Old Testament, *Genesis: 35-47*

submissive to Joseph because God had blessed Joseph with much more than he could ever have imagined.

Joseph had been lied about and mistreated numerous times, yet he held onto his faith in his one true God: Jehovah. He didn't allow circumstances to cause him to take his eyes off of God, the author and finisher of *our* faith *(Heb. 12:2).*

Sometimes, I too feel trapped and hopeless as Joseph must have; yet every time I see a butterfly, it reminds me that God loves me, and that He's sending me something beautiful to fly across my path and brighten my day. It's as if God were presenting me with a present. He bestows so many little blessings on us that sometimes we don't even notice them.

So, if you're feeling as if God just doesn't hear you through all of the tears you've shed, trust me, He hears, and, if you hold onto His promises, your reward is on its way; *"...but those that wait upon the Lord, they shall inherit the earth" (Ps. 37: 9).*

When God tells you that *you can,* don't allow anyone to tell you that *you can't*. God will never leave us or forsake us. He's right there saying, "I acknowledge you and better things are coming."

Where's the Faith?

"...Building up yourself on your most holy faith" (Jude 1:20)

Why are some people afraid to exercise their faith? We often say: "You can be saved;" "You can be healed;" "You can have success," or "Just believe!" But, *is* that enough?

Could it be that when a *miracle* happens, and we don't see, hear, or feel the *manifestation*[2] right away, we fail to believe that it was actually a miracle? We expect things to be *instantaneous*. What happened to *faith*, which is the substance of things hoped for?

Do we enjoy holding onto our situations or conditions because we've made ourselves comfortable with them? Is it because we say, "I was born with asthma (or another health issue), and I'm doomed to suffer with the afflictions the rest of my life?" Have we ever said, "You must be like your mother, she suffered with that disease for years"? Do we also hinder our blessings by saying, "You are the same as…"? No! We are *all* unique. We are *all* our Father's children yet distinct and individual beings. If we should be like anyone, it should be Jesus. *"Be ye therefore perfect, even as your Father which is in heaven is perfect"* (*Mat. 5:48*).

The Bible

What is the Bible? It is the inspired and written Word of God. The Bible is a compass, a treasure map, a key, a recipe, and a way out of trouble when there seems to be no way out. Life is a maze. The Bible contains the directions for getting out of the maze. You don't have to keep bumping into a wall or hedge. You don't have to be *lost*. The Bible is for the righteous and for the

---

[2] a manifest indication of the existence or presence or nature of some person or thing

unrighteous. The Word of God will help a person who sins get their life right. A sinner should want to know what the promises of God are, just as the saint should. The Bible shows each person, who desires to know the truth, how to obtain God's promises.

Paying Prayer to the Holy Spirit

Christ's dying on the cross for our sins led to a "No charge" debt. Jesus paid it *all.* We are also not charged by the Holy Spirit for any of His blessings. So why should we be paying a local newspaper any money to print a prayer which guarantees that our every wish will come true if we submit the ad, pray for three days, and get someone else to do likewise. In recent times, I've seen numerous ads in the newspaper entitled, "*Prayer to the Holy Spirit.*"

God hears our prayers, and He answers them in His time. There are no bargains that we have to make. We must do as the Bible says, "*Be ye holy; for I am holy,*" "*Ask, and it shall be given you,*" "*Whatsoever ye shall ask the Father in my name, he will give it you,*" and so on throughout God's Word. Nowhere does it say that we have to believe in superstitions and pay a newspaper to run a certain prayer ad. I don't think that the Holy Spirit is on anyone's particular paper route. We have a direct line to our Father. Read the Word and get the real story on the "How-to's."

Reading the Bible

Have you ever noticed how you can begin to read your Bible, or any type of inspirational material, and your mind will drift away to "Never-never Land" or somewhere else? You may have looked at two pages, and, when you were finished, you couldn't remember anything about the subject matter. Same thing with *sleep*. It usually hits hard when you're reading the Word. That's Satan attacking you and attempting to keep you from God's promises in the Bible.

Whenever this happens, just catch yourself and start over from where you remember that you left off. Make an extra effort to either read at another time or in another location (get out of bed), but get some Bible reading in each day (even if it's not a whole chapter), and watch how much more you'll accomplish next time. By all means, be faithful. Also, if you're having trouble falling asleep, start reading Psalms. It's the best sleeping pill in the world.

Interpretation

When we read the Bible, it's as if Jesus says, "You can quote me, but don't quote me wrong.

God Bless You

God blesses us through the intervention of man. When we least expect it, God uses a man—friend, neighbor, or stranger—as His hands, feet, or voice to bestow blessings upon us.

Shout

Why we *shout*—deliverance, joy, *defeat* of the devil. If we are tempted and succeed in avoiding the temptation then it's a time to *shout*. When we get a deliverance from an illness; then that's a time to shout. When God has blessed us beyond measure, then we should shout to the Lord in thanksgiving.

Never Let Them See You Sweat

Even television evangelists have trials and tests in their lives. They let you see them in victory; otherwise, if they display defeat, how can they possibly win anybody over for Christ? Yet sometimes they experience hard times, too. Sometimes the world wants to see them fail in order to discredit Christianity. People often use a saint's downfall as the reason for why they don't, or won't, give their lives over to Christ, or as an excuse for why they continue to sin. Even if you, as a Christian representing Christ, don't feel like it just put on a happy face, and trust in God and never let them see you sweat.

What's A Blessing?

Each person is given a different degree or portion of blessings (gifts) from God. If all people received the same gift, you wouldn't be able to recognize your gift when you got it. What might be considered a blessing to one individual may not be a blessing for another person. If you were a plumber, would you want your blessing to be a new set of chef's tools?

We recognize our blessings at different times in our lives—the birth of a baby, purchasing a new home, a marriage, graduating from school, and etc. As we reflect on our lives, we realize how God's hand has shown mercy in our lives each and every time He bestowed His blessings. However, some people never realize that they are being blessed. They ignore the good in their own lives and become angry at the good they see in others' lives. Often, that person is blind to God's blessings, and that is where we (righteous people) come in. We are obliged to help others see their own blessings.

Boy, Am I Lucky

We Christians do not believe in *luck* but in the blessings of our Lord and Savior, Jesus Christ. God does nothing by *chance*. I am blessed to be a blessing.

Music

If the music that you listen to is not edifying, inspiring, uplifting, or encouraging, then it's probably not worth listening to. Music doesn't have to contain *profanity* for it to make an *impact*. There is nothing wrong with some different types of music either such as classical, contemporary, pop, jazz, gospel, rap, hip-hop, rock and roll, or heavy metal, yet we must watch what we put into our spirit.

What we must do is to watch the lyrics. If the lyrics don't make sense, why listen to it? If there is profanity in the lyrics, then you and/or your children don't need to be listening to that particular type of entertainment. If the words of the song tell you to do, think, or act unseemly, then it's not nourishing or proper for your ears. *"Finally, brethren, whatsoever things are true, whatsoever things are honest, whatsoever things are just, whatsoever things are pure, whatsoever things are lovely, whatsoever things are of good report; if there be any virtue, and if there be any praise, think on these things" (Phil. 4:8).*

I'm a music fan of the soulful sounds from the 60s and early 70s. The music back then had a message, and today you'll hear some of those songs in movies. Not all the music was good, but those questionable songs have been filtered out through the years and they didn't withstand the test of time to be classified as, *classics*. This is not to say that those unseemly recordings are not still holding a place in some people's music libraries. Even if you don't listen to them any more, get rid of them. Don't sell them to someone else who might be influenced, but *destroy* them. The same thing goes for certain videos and books. Again, if the music you're listening to is not soothing, comforting or uplifting, TRASH IT! and fine-tune your discernment.

Some of Those Who Walked Before God

Adam *(Gen. 3:8)*
Enoch *(Gen. 5:22, Heb. 11:5)*
Noah *(Gen. 6:9)*
Abraham *(Gen. 17:1, 24:40)*
Levite Priests *(Num. 1:50-53)*
Hezekiah *(II Kings 20:3)*
David *(Ps. 16:8, 116:9. 128:1)*
Micah *(Mic. 6:8)*
Levi *(Mal. 2:6)*
Jesus *(Mat. 3:17)*

Are we walking w*ith* God as these men did? How do we walk upright before God? We should live according to His laws on a continual basis, not just two hours on a Sunday, when we feel like it, or when we think about it, but all during the day and night. Let's make a comparison:

	Shepherd	**Tent Maker**
Biblical Times	Keeps sheep together Watches for Predators Herds sheep to market Sells sheep Sheers the sheep for wool to weave, and trade	Measures and Sews fabrics Talks with co-workers Talks with customers Eats some lunch Buys materials to make tents
	Bus Driver	**Airline Pilot**
Modern Day Times	Keeps eyes on road Drives defensively Remembers route Eats lunch Greets the passengers	Checks the instruments Converses with cabin mates Flies the airplane Talks to the passengers Uses the restroom

People in the old and new testaments didn't have any more or less time to commune with God, but they made the time available. Just as they did, we have to *make* and *take* the time. Do you believe that the men and women of long ago managed their time better than we do today?

Men and women worked for a living then, just as we do today, and, for those of you who venture to say that women have a different role in today's society, consider one New Testament woman in particular, Lydia *(Acts 16:13-15)*. Now there was a *shrewd*[3] *businesswoman.* Who is to say that this woman did not have a family? She *did* have a household. She probably had to go to the market for groceries, cook, clean if she didn't have a staff to assist her around her home, hold or attend prayer meetings, take care of her family (if any), and then go back to the marketplace the next day, to sell her purple cloth to earn her living. *She* took time to be converted to Christianity, and then she offered to be a hostess for the men of God who stopped to teach in her town.

We must put our priorities in order and place God first and foremost in our lives, instead of making up excuses about not having the time to commit to Him. Think about it, and then make some time.

A Wife

A wife – hands you your mother's birthday card and says, "Here Honey, sign this and say something nice to your Mom."

A wife – juggles each day's itinerary with a smile when you tell her—the night before—that you forgot to remind her that she has a dentist appointment at 8:00. She already had another place by 10:00, can't be late for lunch with you at 11:45, has a school meeting at 5:00, a nail appointment at 6:30; the office party at 8:30 (Yes, we do socialize at work. You never know who may need to hear the

---

[3] characterized by keen awareness, sharp intelligence, and often a sense of the practical

Word of God). Isn't it a good thing she planned that hair appointment yesterday, told Sue she'd go shopping with her next week, picked up a few groceries yesterday after work, and tomorrow just happens to be her day off from work? Amazing!!!

A wife – reminds you that you do have children and will let you know their names and ages when you ask.

A wife – makes cookies the night before for her sons second-grade school party which she is supposed to be attending, walks her preschooler to the bus, comes home and does her daily devotional as she waits for a load of clothes to finish, picks up the mail, takes the clothes to the cleaners, picks up her preschooler from the bus stop, makes dinner, gets ready for a women's meeting, and listens attentively while her spouse tells her of his busy day.

A wife – has super-sensitive hearing, which lets her know when someone in the house calls out during the middle of the night, and built-in ear plugs to disregard the snores.

A wife – may not be the same size as she was when you met, but she continues to be the attractive beauty you married some years ago.

A wife – tells you she loves you and will stand by your side till earthly *death do you part.*

When all is said and done, a wife – takes all this in stride, loves every moment, and wouldn't trade her life with anyone.

Didn't You See Me?

Why is it, when people owe you money, or didn't return something that they may have borrowed, they tend to shy away from you or ignore you completely? Is it because of their conscience, or would they like to sever their relationship with you in hopes of clearing their debt by assuming that in time, you will forget it?

Does the Church Have a "Head Cold"?

The church body is under the attack of the devil, and the church has symptoms like that of the flu *(Isaiah 29:9-15)*.

Symptoms:

Stopped-up head:
Can't hear the Word of God

Eyes swollen shut:
Can't see our faults and sins

Body aches – pains:
Backsliding, backbiting, gossip, hurt by a church member

Coughing and spreading germs:
Sowing discord among the brethren

Itchy, watery eyes:
We can't see the enemy before us

Dizziness:
Can't understand the Word of God

Headaches:
Suffering from attacks of the enemy on our health

Fever:
Hot for the things of this world or anger towards one another

Can't breathe:

Unable to witness to anyone due to a lack of knowledge—not studying the Bible

Relief:

Open our understanding to God's Word and bind up sickness and disease.

Take medication and rest. Rest in the Lord Jesus Christ and have a large dose of the Holy Spirit, our comforter and protector. Let's have some of the fruit of the Holy Spirit.

Pain Reliever: Take a dose of the Word of God. *Listen* to the Holy Spirit instead of just *hearing* Him. Act on the Word and let our light so shine before men. *(Mat. 5:16)*

Virtual Reality

Virtual Reality[4] is a reality. A lot of the images that we see and interact with are of evil intent. There are so many video games that steal, kill and destroy the characters or participants in the game *("The thief cometh not, but for to steal, and to kill, and to destroy: I am come that they might have life, and that they might have it more abundantly" Jn. 10:10)*. What we see through our eyes has a direct influence on our minds and hearts.

We must find a way to introduce this concept to our children in a moral way. You may say, "I'll keep my child from this modern technology." Well, will that attitude be a help or a hindrance to our children? What will happen when they go over to their friend's

[4] A computer simulation of a real or imaginary system that enables a user to perform operations on the simulated system and shows the effects in real time

house and get on their computer? Remember, just as we must do, our children have to survive in this world. They have to adapt and advance in spite of the evil that influences everything.

I can imagine how the earlier Christians felt when they had to deal with change. Radio was probably considered the *work of the devil* at first; and, when TV appeared on the scene, *that* must have been the ultimate end.

We Christians must continue to survive the evils of some modern technology. It's an ongoing cycle. As parents, we shouldn't allow evil game cartridges to creep into our homes. We should teach our child that evil isn't pleasing to God. We should monitor our children's activities wisely. And finally, we should also pray that we and our children go through this phase of development without much conflict, and that we all remain saved.

Horror Stories

Have you noticed how cartoons have become more violent over the years? What happened to the sweet innocence of "Mickey Mouse," the cuteness of "Baby Huey," and the heroism of "Mighty Mouse"?

My stepmother once brought to my attention that all fairy tales have an antagonist, (the evil character) and a protagonist (the good character). These tales could be viewed as horror stories by a young child.

For example, look at "Hansel and Gretel." Here were two innocent little children taken advantage of and almost eaten by a wicked old witch. It's the same thing with "The Three Little Pigs" and the big bad wolf, and "Little Red Riding Hood" and the wolf that ate Grandma. Such scary stories to share with a young child, yet most of us have been exposed to all of these stories. Are we exposing our young children to the same kinds of things? They may be classic tales, but don't be surprised if one day there will be a college class on the horror in children's classics.

"Rock-a-Bye-Baby;" what a song we may have sung to our children. "Down will come baby, cradle, and all." Are we wishing harm upon our children? No, I am not taking things to an extreme, but we must watch what goes into the child because it is the by-product of what will come out of them. We've been programmed to pass on traditional rituals of reciting literature without really thinking about what we're truly saying.

Before introducing them to this particular form of literature or song, we should wait until our children are old enough to understand and reason for themselves. It's helpful learning these handed down customs especially if you want to play "Trivial Pursuit," "Jeopardy," or "Name That Tune."

Lifting Holy Hands

When some people worship the Lord, they have different styles of raising their hands to worship. Allow me to explain some of those positions. If someone is robbing you, and they tell you to, "Stick up your hands;" you would raise them as high as they tell you with your palms turned outwards. You would, in other words, "Reach for the sky." That would be a position of surrender. We are expected to give the thief what they demand from us. In church, we raise our hands high because we are not ashamed of God, and it is God who gives us the ability to raise our limbs anyway. *"For I am not ashamed of the gospel of Christ: for it is the power of God unto salvation to every one that believeth; to the Jew first, and also to the Greek" (Rom. 1:16).*

There is another way that people might raise their hands to God, and that is with palms facing up and arms stretched out (as if one was to carry a load). This is a gesture of an offering. We are giving all of our praise and worship as a sacrifice. It is an offering up to the Lord as sweet incense to Him and Him alone.

Some people may do a wave towards the heavens. Hands held high palms facing forward and waving from side to side. It's like a waving homage to the King of Kings. It's just like the people of Hawaii, who speak with their hands and body when they dance, a story is told.

One last expression of adoration is with arms raised, and palms facing each other. It's like a child who offers their hand to grab their parents' hand to cross a street. There is safety in that outstretched hand. Outstretched hands show an expression of love to our Father. Can you imagine reaching up to God, and believing that God is reaching back with outstretched hands to us? With our hands in this acknowledgement, we let God know that we depend upon Him for everything. He is our Elohim (the God who is the Creator). He is El Shaddai (the All-Sufficient One). We should praise Him as El Elyon (the Most High God). Our Lord is called El Olam (the Everlasting God). We should know Him as Adonai (Lord, Master). He is Qanna (a Jealous God). Worship Him as Jehovah-Nissi (the Lord my Banner); Jehovah-Raah (the Lord my Shepherd); Jehovah-Jireh (the Lord Will Provide); Jehovah-Rapha (the Lord that Healeth); Jehovah-Shalom (the Lord is Peace); Jehovah-Shammah (the Lord is There). Let us esteem Him as Jehovah-Sabbaoth (the Lord of Hosts); Jehovah-Tsidkenu (the Lord our Righteousness), and Jehovah-Mekoddishkem (the Lord Who Sanctifies you).[5]

When I read Rev. Kenneth E. Hagin's book entitled *"Plans, Purposes and Pursuits,"* I recalled the section on reverence. Just as in *Ecc. 3:1-8*, there is a time to clap your hands, but, usually in a church setting, it's also a time to raise holy hands. As Rev. Hagin stated, "The world claps, saints praise." No matter what the position, do it and lift your hands up as unto the Lord.

Raise Your Hands If You're Sure

Why do some people raise one or two hands in church when a preacher or a pastor in a church says something?

[5] "Lord I Want To Know You", a devotional study of the Names of God, by Kay Arthur; Fleming H. Revell Co., Old Tappan, N.J.

Christians raise their hands to give praise to God the Father Almighty and to acknowledge Him for all that He has done for them. Some Christians raise only one hand in confirmation that they are in agreement of what is being said. It's a "Count me in," affirmation or a vote of assurance.

Also if you've ever wondered, the reason that someone may ask you to reach your hands out towards Sister So-and-So is because the person praying is asking you to extend your Faith (or your hands) to their prayer. *"Again I say unto you, That if two of you shall agree on earth as touching any thing that they shall ask, it shall be done for them of my Father which is in heaven" (Mat. 18:19).*

The Gifts of the Spirit — Promises of God

(*I Cor. 12: 4-10*)

Word of Wisdom	Working of Miracles
Word of Knowledge	Prophecy
Faith	Discerning of Spirits
Gifts of Healing	Diverse Kinds of Tongues

Interpretation of Tongues

"*A man's gift maketh room for him, and bringeth him before great men*" (*Prov. 18:16*).

If we desire a gift from the Holy Spirit, we must *ask* and *pray* for that gift. If you have not received, it is probably because you asked not, so you received not or maybe because you asked amiss.[6]

[6] *James.4: 2-3*

We also must watch *what* gifts we ask for and *how* we ask for our gifts. Find out what is entailed when you receive a gift before asking for one. Some of the gifts reveal, some have power, and some have the ability to tell the recipient something. The gifts of the Spirit are sometimes to benefit us, but they are usually given to us in order to *help* someone else. They're the *"Gifts that keep on giving."*

Let's not limit God's giving us any of these gifts by tying His hands due to our sinning. Do we ever refuse a gift or a present? No; and we shouldn't. We should desire gifts—especially those that come from God. *"Every good and perfect gift comes from above" (James.1: 17).* All gifts (blessings) are from above. *"A man can receive nothing, except it be given him from heaven" (John 3: 27).* Yes, even a material gift from Aunt Sookie is a blessing. She was blessed to be able to get it, and then she blessed you with it.

Concerning the *Operations of the Gifts of the Spirit,* at different times, we can operate in different gifts through Jesus Christ, by the Fathers' will. *(I Cor. 12:7-11)* There are 3 types of the 9 supernatural gifts of the Holy Spirit. The Revelation Gifts: *A Word of Knowledge* is supernatural revelation, by the Holy Spirit, of certain facts in the mind of God; a *Word of Wisdom* is divine insight into things that are to come; and the *Discerning of Spirits* which enables those persons to be able to see into the Spiritual realm. Then there are The Power Gifts: *Faith* which is a supernatural believing in things that cannot be seen; *Miracles* are supernatural acts or events of power that would defy or go against our natural laws; and *Healing* which is the superior acts of power that would make an individual healthy without natural means. The Inspirational Gifts: *Prophecy* is a message given to someone in order to edify, exhort or comfort the individual; *Tongues* is an unknown language that is spoken by a person through the inspiration of the Holy Spirit; and *Interpretation of Tongues* which is the gift granted to man by God to understand portions of what is spoken to and from God in an unknown language.

Now, on the subject of the *Interpretation of Tongues*: There *isn't* always an interpretation from someone when tongues go forth. Sometimes the Holy Spirit is making intercession to the Father on our behalf. We don't know unless the Spirit reveals those things to us. Again we may ask, but may not really want, or have a need to know. One must *be still* and listen for the voice of God, and then do as unctioned (led) by the Holy Spirit. Just as *water baptism* is an outward sign of an inward change, *speaking in tongues*, as the Holy Spirit gives utterance, is the evidence of the infilling of the Holy Spirit within us. It is a way to talk directly to God.

Let's desire and accept these precious Gifts of the Holy Spirit that God has so graciously given to us who desires them.

Hear – Understand – Do

"I hear from God, but I don't understand what He's saying." Why? Sometimes it's not meant for us to understand at that particular time.

Know — knowledge. You must build knowledge through reading, research, or by asking questions. It just doesn't happen overnight. You can pray for, and receive a *Word of Knowledge*, and it will come to you at an appointed time. *Word of Knowledge* is supernatural revelation, by the Holy Spirit, of certain facts from the mind of God. It is the God-given ability to receive from God, by revelation, the facts concerning something that is humanly impossible for us to know anything about. A "word" of knowledge is just a part of God's insight (omniscience) regarding a specific situation or incident.[7]

When God gives us an assignment, it is our responsibility to GO and DO. If we don't complete our assignment, then God will use another more willing vessel. When God said to, "Occupy until I come;" He meant we are to be content, but not complacent. Don't say, "I'm going to stay put until the rapture comes, and I'm not moving another inch further." What happened to our Lord's command to us, through that *Word of Knowledge*, when He commanded to us to "Go and teach"? We must not just be *hearers* but also *doers* of God's Word.

No Clue

Some of God's people don't know what it means to be *Born Again.* They have been raised in holiness, but have yet to experience

---

[7] (see "The Gifts of the Spirit — Promises of God")

the true joy of holiness themselves. The time has come for this generation to merit the grace of God on their own instead of riding on the prayer shirttails of their parents.

"For many are called, but few chosen." (Mat. 22:14) "...The harvest truly is plenteous, but the laborers are few." (Mat. 9:37)

We cannot help save everyone but we can show people the way, yet God gives every human being the chance and the choice of being *Born Again.* We need to encourage the lost to seek God for their personal salvation. God will listen to everyone's prayers. It's up to them how He answers.

Don't Be Hard-Hearted

Pharaoh's heart was hardened over ten times when he was confronted by Moses to let God's people go.[8] All of the Egyptian's hearts were hardened as well. It wasn't until the angel of death passed over their town that the Egyptians and Pharaoh recognized the power of the one true God of Moses.

The desire to do *right* or *wrong* is placed in us via our conscience. God gives each one of us the opportunity to do what's right, or we can choose to do what is unpleasing to Him *"...choose you this day whom you will serve, ...but as for me and my house, we will serve the Lord" (Joshua 24:15).* God wants us to have the very best, and, if we do what is right, we won't have to go through the plagues that the

[8] Plagues and disasters for Egypt (*Exodus 7:3, 7:13, 7:14, 7:22, 8:19, 9:12, 9:35, 10:20, 10:27, 11:10* and *14:4*)

Egyptians endured by being hard-headed and hard-hearted. Don't allow the enemy to harden your heart towards the things of God.

The Tongue

If you didn't hear something directly from the horse's mouth, (i.e., "Mary said that you looked flat chested in that outfit you wore last Sunday"), and, if your statement won't help the person you are telling, keep it to yourself and avoid gossip. There are seven things that the Lord can't stand, and someone who spreads strife is one of them.[9] *"The tongue can no man tame; it is an unruly evil, full of deadly poison" (James. 3:8).* We can, though, watch what and how we say things that come out of our mouths.

Remember, the movie *Bambi*? Thumper said, "If you can't say something nice, then don't say anything at all." There's a lot of wisdom in this and many of the old Walt Disney cartoon movies.

Fantasia was another cartoon movie that religious folks wanted to and did condemn. Some people said the movie portrayed too much evil. If we watch the cartoons and shows with our children and explain what is going on, they will learn, through our explanations, the difference between good and evil and right and wrong. We must be there to teach and guide our children. Are we guilty of using the TV as a baby-sitter, or are we explaining the concept to our children that, "good, can and does triumph over evil?"

---

9 *Prov.6: 16-19*

Yes, I do watch television and sometimes go to movies; however, I am very selective as to what my household and I watch. Learn to discern and be selective. It may be on, but you don't have to watch it. Also, weekly shows do not have to be watched every week. People, who cannot attend church because their "XYZ" program is on, should not be *slaves* to their TV sets or its programs. Tape the show until you can be delivered from its bondage but go to church as you should.

Speak…

…Boldly …good things …well of others …the truth …Christ (in the name of Jesus) …from the heart via your mouth …with wisdom …and speak freely with the power of the Holy Ghost.

The pen and tongue are mightier than any sword *(Prov. 18:21 and James.3: 5-11).* There is great power in that little member that we have in our mouths. How is your opening? Is the flavor that is coming out bitter or sweet? I must tell you right now, don't repeat anything around me that I can't share with my best friend because, I *must* tell Jesus.

Busy, Busy, Busy

A Christian's telephone line should never be busy unless they are praying with someone, conducting business, on a long-distance call (when we can afford to be), or counseling another person under the direction of the Holy Spirit. Don't get upset. You know I'm right. ☺

Help Wanted

The church body needs *many* people to volunteer their help. We may use the excuse that we don't want to be used to work in the church because one of our family members is already represented. "Daddy Grace is on the deacon board. Isn't that enough?"

How do you think God should react to the person who refuses to help out? Wouldn't it be something if God selected just one member to represent our family in heaven? Who do you think would be *His* first choice? Could you be certain it would be you? We all need to get busy!

Hearsay

"I heard it from the horse's mouth." Even when you know the whole story, not even then can you pass judgment about the person or the information. Get the whole story from the source and then pray. And remember, there are always two sides to every story.

Saved – Or Being Judgmental?

"Look at her. And she calls herself a child of God." Who are we to say if someone is saved or not saved? Are we God? Do we know the thoughts of that other person or the thoughts of God? Even if a man continues to sin, who are we to say that God is not able to forgive that person? He is a God of mercy. Are we to say who *is* forgiven and who *is not* forgiven?

A person may <u>not</u> be living a good example, as a model Christian should be, but should we condemn that person with criticism from our mouths? The Bible says, *"Judge not, that ye be not judged" (Mat. 7:1)*, and *"For if we would judge ourselves, we should not be judged. But when we are judged, we are chastened of the Lord, that we should not be condemned with the world" (I Cor. 11:31-32).* We can be hopeful and prayerful that the person will yield himself totally to God before it's too late. Only God knows the person's heart.

Don't go by what it may look like. Appearances are not always accurate. God could be doing a work (changing the person from the inside out) right at that very moment. Just anticipate the best for that person and walk in love. We can be an *example* to people by being *good ambassadors* for Christ.

What is salvation or being saved? It is the day of awakening or becoming conscious to the reality of real life—eternal life—through Jesus Christ, who gave His life for us so that we could share that eternal life. Being saved is the deliverance, when we repent, from the destruction that we have earned because of our sins.

What's On Sale?

Young people today are wearing just about anything. Sometimes it's too tight, much too short, too revealing (leaving nothing to the imagination) or it's dropping off their butt to reveal underwear that your grandpa wouldn't wear. Are our young people (and some old folks who should know better) hanging themselves out like an old "For Sale" sign that is tattered, worn, and torn? Why aren't they encouraged to be the apple of God's eye? Would He be proud to call them His children? Here's a new slogan: What Would Jesus Wear? (WWJW?)

In God's eyes, we Christians are gems. We are people who should be looked up to as examples of Christ. We are not elevating the physical man but that spiritual likeness of Christ that is nestled inside of us. As heirs to the throne, and children of the King, we must carry ourselves as such and walk with our heads held high, with *Great Expectations*,[10] and not settle for less than our Father would expect from us.

Pennies From Heaven

When you owe somebody money, and you don't pay them back, don't consider it to be a blessing from the Lord. If that person *wants* to give you money or a personal possession, they'll let you know. Pay back what you owe others without them having to ask you for it. If you don't have it at the time you agreed to repay the debt, let the person know when they may expect it. Don't avoid that person like the plague. Forgetting a debt is one thing. Manifesting a "blessing" for *yourself* is another

[10] *Great Expectations* by Charles Dickens

Humility

What does it mean to be *poor in spirit*? It means to be *humble* in your spirit man. It doesn't mean that you don't have a dime in your pocket and it doesn't mean that you are trod down by the events of life, either. A person who is *poor in spirit* is a person who is *teachable*. *"Blessed are the poor in spirit: for theirs is the kingdom of heaven" (Mat. 5:3).*

Dancing Machine

Just because someone says that they are "dancing in the spirit" doesn't mean that the person has the Holy Ghost. I've had my foot trampled on by someone who claimed to be "dancing under the influence of the Holy Ghost."

When you dance in the spirit, you *will* continue to have control of your body. You won't be thrashing around and losing your bodily functions. The Holy Spirit is a gentleman and He dwells in you. When you receive the infilling of the Holy Spirit, He is part of your spirit man. He knows you, and you know Him. Sometimes you will feel so blessed, so thankful for all that God has done in your life that the feeling makes you want to sing, praise Him, and yes, even dance.

Communion

(*I Cor. 11:23-30*)

Communion is a time to partake of Our Lord's body and blood (bread & wine symbolism). It's a sharing of a close personal moment that builds up our spirit man, until we get the chance to partake again.

Why is it taught, in some churches, that we should *not* partake, one with another, of our Lord's Supper at another church, or with a different body of believers within the body of Christ? *"For as often as ye eat this bread, and drink this cup..." (I Cor. 11:26).* As Christians, aren't we all sisters and brothers with the same Father? *"There is neither Jew nor Greek, there is neither bond or free, there is neither male nor female: for all are one in Christ Jesus" (Gal. 3:28).*

I've taken communion at a Catholic funeral, and there was NO sin committed by doing this act. This is not a doctrine but a *command* from Christ. The commemorative act was proclaimed so that each and every one of us would build ourselves up (become spiritually stronger) in the mighty name of God.

Praise/Worship

Praise silences the devil. *Praise* comes from the mouth. *Praise* is a garment of our spirit man. *Praise* leads the believer into the triumph over disruptive situations through Christ. *Praise* brings revelation. *Praise* prepares us for miracles. God inhabits our praises, *"But thou are holy, O thou that inhabitest the praises of Israel" (Ps. 22:3)*, and He brings us into His presence. Praise is a *sacrifice*, an *offering*, to our most high God. It is *not* supposed to be a ritual or a chore.

What is *worship*? *Worship* is giving honor and glory to God, our Father. It is unselfish praise. *Worship* is not thinking, "What will I get out of it?" but thinking, "What can I *give* to God?" It's a one-on-one direct flow of adoration from us directly to God, our Father.

More on Praise and Worship

There ***is*** a difference between p*raise* and wo*rship.*

Praise is usually a fast-tempo style of music. It is our elevation of joy that is offered up to our Father, God. When we sing a praise song, we are displaying our happiness that we serve such a mighty, merciful, and awesome God.

Worship is an unselfish act of adoration. We get gratitude from swooning our Father, just as two people who are in love would experience, and when we sing worship songs—it's all about Him.

When we attended dances long ago, what type of tempo music was used before everyone was asked to go home ("Last call for alcohol." Don't play like you don't remember). The most common song was "*Good Night Sweetheart*"? It was a slow song.

We shouldn't jerk God around either. Slow then fast, or fast then slow, and then fast again. A *praise and worship leader* has to lead the people into the presence of Almighty God. Worship is adoration. It's a time of reverence and devotion. It's an *ooey-gooey* time of love for God. God is ushered into our presence and when it's time for the Word (sermon, homily, message, lesson or preaching), then His Word will come forth without hindrances.

Choirs and Commitment

If a choir is not dedicated and disciplined, then they will not be effective. When there are no rules, and a member does what he or she wants to, and comes to practice when they choose to, then the other, faithful members become disillusioned and disinterested.

The ministry of serving God in song is not a show-and-tell, or "They need my voice to uplift the congregation" experience. I believe, if a person has not been blessed to sound like BeBe or CeCe Winans, then they can sing out to the Lord in a sweet bouquet of song in their own way. Attitude is most important, especially in remembering to whom we're singing, and what we're singing for.

I have seen the anointing leave a choir over the years due to a haughty spirit within that choir. The Lord will bless our endeavors to a certain point. We have to do our part: Come to rehearsal on time, be devoted to the ministry, be committed, and be faithful. This is what God expects from us when we sing and everyone will be blessed.

Forgiven

Even before you did that which you had intended to do (sin), God knew your intents, and He blessed you, and blessed you, and blessed you, in spite of—you. If you ask for forgiveness, then He will forgive you.

To Have and To Hold

Enjoy your spouse, and don't just tolerate him or her. Each of us has different good or bad days, and we need to be understanding when our mate is having a bad day and lift him/her up in prayer for deliverance from whatever is bothering him/her. If you are unevenly yoked (i.e., a Christian married to a non-Christian), pray, with your hand upon your spouse, "Thank you Lord for my Christian wife/husband."; the same thing would apply to you and your children. Place your hands gently on them and pray that good things will come upon them. This actually works.

We Must Work, While It Is Day

I have heard and seen some pastors talk about calling it quits after so many years. God has no retirement plan here on earth, or in the earth (speaking of ourselves as earth). *"The earth is the Lord's, and the fullness thereof; the world, and they that dwell therein" (Ps. 24:1).*

We may want to change positions such as going from being a pastor to a motivational speaker, but not give up doing a work for God, and, most importantly, make sure that *it is* the will of God. We should continue to work in the ministry of Christ for as long as we live. If you decide to be a salesman or engineer, then please don't leave your ministry tools in the garage. Take your tools with you!

Our Children Have To Leave Sometimes (Let Them Go, and Pray)

Envision, if you will, a mother bird teaching her young fledgling to fly. She leads the little bird out of the nest for its first solo flight. Mama bird has taught the young one well. She turns him loose and hopes that he uses his learned skills. Suddenly, here comes helpful neighbor bird who wants to save the little one. The neighbor bird grabs the young one and doesn't allow him to experience flight on his own. Neighbor bird means well, but the young bird now doesn't want to fly on his own or leave the nest. Mother bird has to start all over again.

"Train up a child in the way he should go: and when he is old, he will not depart from it" (Prov. 22:6).

As parents, we too must allow our children to leave the nest. Neighbors and friends still need to watch out for a child's welfare, yet be careful to help out—*only* with the agreement of the parent—if or when the child goes astray.

By all means, if a vulture comes to harm the young fledgling (or child), *please do* come and rescue the defenseless one. Now when all is well, please dear neighbor, allow the young bird to grow up and be his own bird.

God, Our Parent

When a child is young, he clings to his mother. As the child grows, he sometimes drifts away and wants to be with his peers or go out on his own. Parents are sometimes the last people he wants to be near. As the child gets older and enters maturity, he yearns to be closer to the ones who cared for him, nurtured him, tolerated his moods, and who loved, and guided him. So too will God our Father do with us. He waits for us to mature and to realize that it is He who loves us, and, in the process, His love, care, and patience never fail.

Until they leave this earth, parents are always (or should always be) there for their children. We must watch that we don't let Christ be dead to us due to our sins, which separate us from God's love. It's never too late to get close to your parents, either heavenly or earthly.

Home Alone

We're living in a day when more and more children are left at *home alone* ("Latch-key" kids). We, as parents, cannot be too cautious. When left alone—sometimes it can't be helped, but never should a young child be left unattended—our children should be instructed *never* to let anyone into the house, not even if it is Jesus. That may sound sacrilegious, but we continue to face times when more and more men are being deceivers *("But evil men and seducers shall wax worse and worse, deceiving, and being deceived" II Tim. 3:13)*, and our unprotected children are being violated. Our society has become so perverted that we really need to be as wise as a serpent yet as harmless as a dove *(Mat. 10:16)*.

Being Critical

Critique, <u>don't</u> *criticize*. When weighing a situation, the questions that we should ask ourselves should be, "Why is the good, good? How do I make the better even better? Where is Jesus in this particular situation? Do we need to add a little more Jesus?"

Why don't we tell people, "I love the Jesus in you"? Now, if Jesus isn't there, I'll love the person anyway, and hope that He will be manifested in their life very soon. "Let's find Jesus in others, and, hopefully, let others see that He's showing up in our lives too."

"We" vs. "I"

We know that we can do all things through Christ who strengthens us *(Phil. 4:13)*, and that we are not much without God *(I John 4:4)*, and that it's better to have the Holy Ghost in us than to be without Him *(Rom. 15:13)*; therefore, why confuse people by saying "we" when speaking of ourselves?

Did Jesus not say, in *Matthew 18:20, "...there am I in the midst of thee"?* Paul used the pronoun "I" in many references to himself: *"For I am not ashamed of the Gospel" (Rom. 1:16); "Wherefore I was made a minister...." (Eph. 3:7),* or *"I press toward the mark..."* (*Phil. 3:14*) and *"I can do all things..."* (*Phil. 4:13*). We aren't being boastful by utilizing the correct pronoun. We are only making ourselves clear. "*I* am receiving a healing, and *I* will be feeling better in Jesus name."

The world and some Christians are confused enough as it is. Why not say, "I am doing this . . . through the power of Christ", or "I will arrive at the meeting at noon." When a person refers to himself as we, I'm usually trying to figure out about whom else the person is speaking instead of paying attention to what he/she is saying.

"We" vs. "I" (Part II)

When speaking to people, identify who you're addressing and don't confuse them. If you say we, it should be you and another person (i.e., we, my husband and I; or we, the Poller's, or we, the members of the church board). The Preamble[11] of the Constitution begins by identifying who the "we" is that the document refers to: "We, the people of the United States…"

If I'm speaking just about myself, I'll say "I," and I shouldn't be afraid of sounding boastful or improper. I can't assume the world will know that the "we" of whom I speak of is the *Holy Spirit* within me and *me*.

Be Positive

If we say, "We *don't*," then eventually "We *won't*." We must be positive in all that we say and do. The devil will tell you that, "You *can't*," but you must say "I *can*." *"I can do all things through Christ who strengthens me" (Phil. 4:13).*

What Is A Testimony?

A testimony is something that serves as evidence. A testimony is edifying or uplifting the name of God. It is giving a good report of the goodness that God has done for you. A testimony is a statement given to uplift the other saints around you, after it has uplifted you.

God Does Not Argue

We may try to justify or find fault with what God wants us to do when we read the Bible. And sometimes we just refuse to accept His commands and we do our own thing.

---

[11]an introductory statement; preface; introduction

When God says to repeat a *"Word of Knowledge"* or a *"Word of Wisdom"* to someone, we should comply. If the person doesn't want to accept the Word, then our work as the messenger has been done. We, as the messengers, completed the work on our end; it's up to the receiver and God to do the rest, but, if we don't deliver, there is always someone else who will do what God asks.

Heaven

What is heaven? Heaven is the residence or home of God, the angels, and the spirits of the righteous after death; the place or state of existence of the blessed after the mortal life.[12]

Well, what is your heaven? Let's focus. What has God said that heaven will be like?[13] Do you want to go? We're going to have a party and all the saints of God will be there. "I won't be disappointed; He promised me a lot of great things!"

Heaven will have no denominations nor will there be a separate section for a particular religious sect (no Pentecostal row, no Baptist corner, or a Catholic hood). We will be one people and He will be our one God. Blessed be His glorious name.

Our job, while we are here on earth, is to win souls (other people) for heaven. We should desire to have our children, parents, siblings, neighbors, and co-workers (yes, even the rotten ones) join

---

[12] http://dictionary.reference.com/browse/heaven
[13] See Revelations chapters 21 and 22

us in heaven. People's spirits have no color distinction, no particular class, or position in life (laborer, CEO, banker, farmer, minister, and etc.) when they go to heaven.

Sincere, Or Not Sincere

"I thank God who is the head of my life." Has this become a popular phrase to the world for those who don't know who God is? Do celebrities, who receive awards on the "Grammy's" or other award shows, ever thank the pastors from the churches that they attend? Where do they think their talent came from? It came from God, not their managers, staff members, production crews, song writers, producers or the local sponsors!

Thank You…For What?

"In all thy ways acknowledge him, and he shall direct thy paths" (Prov. 3:6).

"Thank you Jesus." "Thank you Jesus." "Thank you Jesus." "Thank you Jesus." "Thank you Jesus." "Thank you Jesus."

This was the phrase that was previously used to invite the Holy Ghost (Spirit) into a person's life. We've learned that the Holy Spirit is a precious gift. He comes willingly to those who request Him. But let's get back to Jesus. "Thank you Jesus."

One morning—very early as it was so customary for the Lord to visit—God whispered to me, "Why do you thank me?" "What are you giving thanks for?"

Why do we sometimes unconsciously repeat, "Thank you Jesus," and that's the end of the sentence. Yes, I too was guilty of saying, "Thank you Jesus." Just a blurb of what I thought was an announcement of appreciation. But what was I being thankful for?

Sure we may say "Thank you" to a person when they hand us something, but the statement is usually said face-to-face and usually right after the kindness is rendered. Example: someone gives you a gift in a pretty package and you say, "Thank you." Later you can write them a little card and express how the gift and their act of kindness really blessed you.

God made it a little clearer to me. It would be just as if you were going to your friends, a relative, or a complete stranger and you say, "Thank you Lou, or Thank you Aunt Tillie, or Thank you dad," and you keep repeating "Thank you _______ (name)," and you say nothing else. Eventually, that person is going to say: "What?" "What did I do?" "Why are you thanking me?"

It's the same thing with God. "Thank you Jesus." Sooner or later He'll want you to tell Him what you're thankful for. "Thank you Jesus for getting me up this morning." "Thank you Jesus for showing my child favor before the court judge." "Thank you Jesus for sending your angels to protect me from that fatal car crash." "Thank you Holy Ghost for your peace that you've given me during this waiting period in my life." It's okay to say "Thank you Jesus," *sometimes*, yet He'd like to hear *why* you are thanking Him.

And please don't say that He is omniscient (all-knowing). Sure He is, but He'd still like to hear why you're thankful, and *you need* to hear (as a reminder) how He has and still continues to bless you again and again. When we take the time to tell Him why we're thankful and what we're thankful for, He appreciates the gesture even more. It's great to be thankful; nevertheless, let's get specific in our gratitude and let it not be just on Thanksgiving Day. You know how Uncle Henry will take twenty minutes to begin to thank the Lord for everything that He's done over the past year. Not good timing with all the growling tummies. Let's take more time to let Jesus know what He's done for us lately.

Waste Not — Want Not

A mature, experienced, open, and knowledgeable mind is a terrible thing to waste. If you are *not* a college graduate or even a high-school graduate, God still has things for you to do. Your mind is not empty, and you can spread the Word of God as well as those who have graduated from some institution. You may just use different means to do so. God will guide you, and you won't be wasting the knowledge that you have.

What Have You Done To Be Tired?

Have you healed the sick? Raised the dead? Given hope to the hopeless? Have you done any of these things in Jesus name? Have you allowed God to get the glory? Yes, all these things Christ did, but did He not say to us and His apostles, that even greater things will we do in His name? *"Verily, verily, I say unto you, He that believeth on me, the works that I do shall he do also; and greater works than these shall he do; because I go unto my Father"* (*John 13:12*).

Operator

We should be in communication with God at all times. What would we do if God had an answering machine? We know He doesn't, but what if? What if we say, "GOD I NEED HELP NOW"? And God says, "I'm unable to speak with you right now, please leave your name, number, and a brief message." Would He remember who we are when we left that message? We may have needed Him that very moment or face the jaws of death. Would we be able to hear from God? Or would there be interference on our telephone line? *("I will therefore that men pray every where, lifting up holy hands, without wrath and doubting" I Tim 2:8).* I am so glad that God does not use an answering machine and He answers "on time"!

He's Always on Call

There's someone I know
With a most tiring job,
He's ever and always on call.

He doesn't just work
From nine until five;
He works every hour of the day.

He's a Jack-of-all trades,
And He's mastered them all;
He can help with whatever you need.

His line's never busy,
should you happen to call;
He uses no answer machine.

He never says "Wait,"
When you call His name,
Nor puts you on 'hold' for awhile.

He's able to answer
Each day of the week;
He has no time off at all.

He's there with solutions
Before you can ask,
Fifty-two weeks of the year.

He touches your life,
In a way He sees fit,
Though His cause is not
always clear.

He never gets mad
And always forgives,
If only you take time to ask.

Three-hundred and sixty-five
Days of the year,
He'll answer, if only you ask

No, He never takes a vacation,
For this, I'm eternally glad;
For where would I be,
Or you--for a fact,
If God ***ever*** took a day off?

© J. R. Moses

Prayer

The Apostles asked Jesus, "Lord, teach us to pray," and at that moment the "Our Father" was born. Long ago, God gave His people a praying spirit. There is a song written by Karen Clark-Sheard that goes like this:

Lord, give me a Praying Spirit, A Praying Spirit.
Lord, help me to say yes: Yes, yes Lord.

A Praying Spirit throughout the day, oh: A Praying Spirit, in every way. A Praying Spirit, so that I might stay. Oh, Lord, I want a Praying Spirit Least I pray, oh Lord. Lord, when I pray, give me what to say. And I want to say yes) yes, yes, yes, yes Lord.[14]

What is prayer? Prayer is communication with, communion with, speaking to, and hearing from God. It's being in His presence and not being alone. It's waiting for an answer and being still enough to hear that answer.

Sometimes, before a speaker gets up to bring forth a message in church, the congregation expects that person to pray a long prayer before he begins to speak. If a person is in communication with God throughout the day, then acknowledgment of the Almighty should be enough. If a long prayer is needed to help a person open the audience's ears and heart to the message that God would have come from the speaker's lips, then so be it. A cascade of prayers may flow for the benefit of the congregation. A speaker should already have been prepared with the knowledge that God is with him or her.

[14] http://www.music-lyrics-gospel.com/

Jonah's Prayer 2:1-10

(A Modern Day Interpretation)

V. 1: Deep in a world of sin and decay, we call upon the Lord for mercy. We may have done something wrong or might have been disobedient.

V. 2: "I need you Lord. I've called on you before, and you heard my cry and answered my call. I'm calling on you Lord. Hear me."

V. 3: "You put me here in this world, to do a job for you. You let me stumble and fall to the lowest low. Trouble is all around me. Bills, pain, suffering and despair. Lord, it *looks* bad."

V. 4: I said, "Lord, where are you? Do you hear me? I've really done it this time. I can't seem to feel you Lord. Will I ever be in your good graces again?"

V. 5: "Where are you Lord? I can't get out of this rut I'm in. I'm being smothered Lord. I can't see my way. I can't get out of the situation I'm in. *Lord*, you know I've tried."

V. 6: "I tried to end it all. I couldn't take it (life) any more, but that wasn't your plan. You wouldn't let me end my life."

V. 7: "At that very moment, when I felt my life slipping away, I prayed to you. I asked your forgiveness. I requested your help, and from your throne, you heard me."

V. 8: "Lord, I know that those persons, who don't look to You for help in their time of need, look to a false god. They have *cut their own throats*. They who look to gods, other than You, and do not adhere to your Word, give up their grace from you."

V. 9: "But from now on, I'll do right Lord. I'll do what I've promised you I'd do. I'll fast; I'll pray; I'll go when and where You tell me to go. No ifs, ands, or buts. *You* are my *only* hope. Others can do what they will Lord, but I will trust in you."

V. 10: God gave His command and Satan had to step back and back off.

What we do with an order from God is up to us. Do we give up when we make a mistake and throw in the towel? Why not ask for God's forgiveness and press-on? It's amazing what trials God is able to deliver us from when we ask.

The Anointing – Falling Under the Power – Slain in the Spirit – or Just a Time Out

Questions:

What is it? The anointing is the power of the Holy Spirit that comes upon a person, or it's the power present in the atmosphere where the Holy Ghost has descended. It's our submission and total surrender to God. It's a one-on-one with God. It's God's power and love coming upon us.

Why do I or don't I get slain? Most of the time it's *fear* that keeps us wondering. We usually fear that with which we are unfamiliar. We don't *do* what we don't *know*. People of Greece eat a lot of *lamb*. If I have never eaten it, I won't know what lamb tastes like. If I haven't *asked* for a piece, I will never *taste* it. It's the same thing with the anointing of the Holy Spirit *("O taste and **see** that the LORD is good: blessed is the man that trusteth in him." Ps. 34:8)*

Is it wrong if I am not slain? "Judge Not!" One must be at ease and in familiar surroundings. It is always easy to receive the "*Gift of the infilling of the Holy Spirit*" when He is present. Have you ever been in a service and there is what people call, a heavy anointing? Some people actually see a cloud or a mist. There is a calm presence in the air, and you can feel the love of God. God's Holy Spirit may come upon you in the comfort of your own home. If we desire to accept God's gift, then we must submit ourselves to Him and be receptive. Just as the Holy Ghost is a *gentleman*, He will *not* force Himself on you. You will not be slain in the spirit while waiting in line at Publix™ or Wal-Mart™.

There are times now and then when I can be at liberty to take a "time out." Where the Spirit of the Lord is, there is liberty and not liberality *("...and where the Spirit of the Lord is, there is liberty" II Cor. 3:17).* Sometimes you have to be in control, and you can't take a time-out under the anointing. Ushers, music ministry, audio & video, alter workers and many others; now is not your time to relax, but it's time to serve.

Will I hurt myself if I fall? The body can be a frail instrument. No, if you are *truly* under His anointing, God will not allow you to be hurt. So why test God? Usually there are *catchers* who assist the physical body down to the floor and allow God to deal gently with the spirit man. And please, don't go through the actions of falling down just because your girlfriend is on the floor.

Altar workers and catchers are to be in position, ready and praying with the person that God is administering His Spirit through. Your hands *do not* have to be on the person being prayed for unless requested by the person who is being used by God (the minister). And please do not touch the anointed minister unless you are really unctioned by the Holy Spirit to do so. Besides being distracting, a touch can draw the anointing out of the anointed person.

I have seen persons fall in slow motion, who have avoided objects (pews, chairs, or other people), when no one was there to catch them. They remained unharmed. Only <u>God</u> could do that. *Angels Were On Assignment*! Women should be in place for the women, and men should be there to catch the men when possible.

So be aware, be ready, be observant, be prayerful, be *saved*, and *don't* be a hindrance to a blessing. Yes, I did say, "Be saved yourself." How can someone expect to minister to someone else if they themselves need help? Have you stayed saved all day? Get right before you come that close to the presence of the Lord.

A person can *shout all over the place* and not possess the Holy Ghost but only *that person* and *God* will know. You will also be able to control your body just as you maintain control of your bladder; you will not be *thrashing around* on the floor while in the Spirit. God is the author of orderliness—not confusion *(I Cor. 14:33)*.

How is it that some people "fall out," and five minutes later a demon has to be cast out of them? The person's *will* was made to submit to the authority of God just as those in Biblical times *(Mat.8:28, Mk.5:15-16, Lk. 8:36, Acts 8:7 to name a few)*. The person had a demon spirit in them (lust, drugs, lying, stealing, etc.), and the anointed Spirit of God could now deal with the evil spirit within.

Remember the man with an unclean spirit in *Luke 4:35? "And Jesus rebuked him, saying, Hold thy peace, and come out of him. And when the devil had thrown him in the midst, he came out of him, and hurt him not."* We are *not* to judge the person, but *trust* the Lord's judgment.

There have been times when the power of God was so strong that even the *catchers*, who caught the people who fell under the anointing, would themselves collapse under the powerful hand of Almighty God. I have seen the anointing have people fall with a domino effect. The *power* of the Lord is *mighty*.

Finally, let that person, who is taking a time out, know that God loves them, you love them, and the church loves them. They should know God loves them by the experience they've just had.

It's wonderful. Give a smile, give a tissue, give a hug, maybe all three, and, by all means, help them to their feet.

Milk vs. Meat

Heb. 5:13-14

A mother nurses or feeds her newborn (born-again Christian). That mom may wean her child from the breast and begin to introduce some whole milk—a little at a time, maybe some *Carnation Evaporated Milk®*. Later on, as the child's diet advances, mom may share some meat from her plate. She'll cut a small piece, chew it up a little, and then give it to the pre-toddler to consume. When the child is old enough to come to the table and dine, mom will still cut up the meat and take out the bone and gristle.[15] A true meat eater (those who are growing in the knowledge of God) desires meat – since milk is not enough. Some adults are babes, and some are mature Christians. Some children desire milk and some are ready to be introduced to meat *("...Man does not live by bread alone, but by every word that proceedeth out of the mouth of God" Mat. 4:4).*

If I am choking on a piece of meat, I hope someone will do the *Heimlich Maneuver*, to help me get the trapped substance out of my throat, so that I might live. The Word of God is to be consumed a little at a time and washed down with a bit of understanding so that we don't get too much at one time and begin to choke.

---

[15] *Spiritual gristle* is that which confuses us about God's Word and other people's actions towards God's Word.

God wants us to get His Word out to His people. We're not just to chew and chew, but we should digest His entire Word. We should consume the entire Bible and not *choke*. We should also share our piece of meat and not be selfish. If we choke once, are we going to give up eating? Certainly not! The same goes for the Word of God; we should not give up at the first verse or section we do not fully understand.

Christianity

Concerning Christianity, you have to jump in with both feet and with your eyes wide open. You can't just test the water. You can't say that one scripture is too hot, and another one is too cold. It's all or nothing. It's either God or the devil. You cannot serve two masters. *"No man can serve two masters: for either he will hate the one, and love the other; or else he will hold to the one, and despise the other. Ye cannot serve God and mammon"* (*Mat. 6:24*).

Backsliding[16] is like a fish jumping out of a fishbowl. Backsliders are people who choose to take themselves away from the sanctity or safety of the bowl. The minister's duty is to teach the Word over and over again and plop the fish back into the bowl.

Looking For Love

People seek love so hard that they follow after anything that appears to portray a ray of hope. There are people in high and low places who send out questionable messages by the way they dress,

[16] To relapse into bad habits, sinful behavior, or undesirable activities

by their music, by their actions, and by what they have to say (or subliminal messages). These people are usually out for themselves and some of your money. They really don't care about you or your welfare. Are you *looking for love in all the right places*?

Entertaining Angels

"Be not forgetful to entertain strangers: for thereby some have entertained angels unawares" (Heb. 13:1).

Can we be sure who may or may not have been an angel in our life? Are we willing to meet our maker—Father God—and debate with Him about who *was* or who *was not* an angel in our lives? Am I an angel who came into your life? Are you an angel in mine? Anything done by an angel-like person is an example of what Jesus would do and how we should act. However, sometimes God uses people who don't appear to us as angelic. Should we ignore such persons if their message is good and untainted? No. We don't know who God may choose to be an angel in our lives. We cannot afford to judge by appearances alone.

What Is A Prophet?

He or she is an inspired speaker, or a person who speaks for God, or a deity, or by divine inspiration. *"And he said, Verily I say unto you, No prophet is accepted in his own country" (Luke 4:24).*

I believe that your *own country* is that place where you are located, be it your hometown, or that place where you are currently abiding. I also believe that if God has something that He desires to say through me, and if I am a willing and obedient vessel; then He *can* and *will* use me just as he can and will use you when He needs you.

If God can use a donkey *(Num. 22: 21-35),* and a rooster *(Luke 22:61),* then He can use me. Will you be willing to heed His call?

Consider Your Ways

Let's consider the Israelites. Are we, the people of today, so perfect that God will not smite us for our actions, our disobedient ways, or our disrespect as He did in the Old Testament days? *(Please read Exodus 16 before you answer).*

Do You Believe…?

…In Miracles?
…In Healing?
…In Asking and Receiving?
…In Trusting God?
…In Listening to Hear God's Voice?
…In Waiting on the Lord?
…In Keeping Christ First in Your Life?
…In Angels? (*Ps. 8:5* and *Heb. 13:2*)
…In the Power of the Holy Spirit?
…In the Mystery of the Blessed Trinity?
…In Life More Abundantly?
…In a Mansion in Heaven?
…In Receiving anything asked In His Name?
…In the fact that you and I are Children of God?

If we believe in these things, then why isn't Christ being *worshiped* as Lord and King in our lives?

Open Your Eyes

The world, as we know and see it, is looking for **hope**. Sometimes even the talk shows will feature segments on hope after disastrous calamities such as Jim Jones;[17] Waco, Texas; date rape; winning the lottery; disastrous hurricanes; the psychic connection, and more.

What is hope? Hope is the feeling that what is wanted can be had or that events will turn out for the best. People say, "I hope to win the lottery;" or "I hope that I won't get sick." But little do they know that Jesus is the only hope.

Look at soap operas. The main reason that people get hooked on them is because the actors' lives are worse than the viewers' lives. A little misery loves company. There is even demon possession being portrayed in these daily soaps. Is that hopeful?

We should pray for a *strong* "Discernment of Spirit" so that we won't be hooked into being glued to the TV on a particular day or night. We should also watch the places that we go into. If it doesn't feel right, and you get a "bad vibe," pay attention to the Holy Spirit and *get out of there*!

On Mon. May 8, 1995 a movie called "Outbreak[18]" aired. Friday of the same week, the E-Bola virus was actually destroying

---

[17] Jonestown, Guyana

[18] Outbreak" starring Dustin Hoffman & Rene Russo, written by Wolfgang Petersen 1995

people in South Africa. Was it a coincidence that the movie was shown before the news aired? All the occurrences were realistic, including the Centers for Disease Control (CDC) and scientists having to dress in hazardous suits, and recently, we haven't heard anything else about the disease. Has it been cured? Think about it!

Michael Landon of *Little House on the Prairie* and *Highway to Heaven* always showed *belief in God.* Could the reason why Michael went home to be with the Lord be that his work here on earth was done? As viewers of his shows, did we listen? Did we see? Did we heed the messages that were brought to our attention through his stories? Michael gave us much to hope for through his productions and storylines.

Another message movie was *Angels in the Outfield*[19]. It does *not* have a lot of gore, murder, sex, or violence (unpopular in these days), but it *does* have a message. It seems that shows with a message have a short season, both on screen and on TV, and corrupt shows quickly squeeze out the wholesome shows. Can we see? And are we hearing the correct message? We're to continue to hope, yet we have to put our trust in God. Keep your eyes on the *prize*.

I Want To Have…

…The Wisdom of Solomon
…The Compassion of Joseph
…The Strength of Samson
…The Leadership of Moses

---

[19] 1994, Walt Disney Pictures, Calif., Dorothy Kingsley & George Wells

...The Humility of Jeremiah
...The Oneness with God as Enoch had
...The Patience of Job (without so many afflictions)
...The Love of Christ

Help!

If you can't pray for help (God's grace and mercy), then please, stop praying for hindrances. Don't *'player hate'*.[20]

Who's The Captain of Your Team?

The devil is after the s*aints* (those who follow the teachings of Christ), not as much as the s*inners* (those who follow after Satan and his demons). He already controls the mind of the sinner, but he keeps an eye on them so as not to lose them to the teachings of the Lord. A person who is not a Christian may say, "I'm not a part of God," but the Lord had a purpose for that person even before he or she was born. It was the person's decision (choice) whether he or she would follow Christ or follow the devil. Who are you going to have as your team captain?

Watch Rationale

There was a pot-blessing dinner at the church hall, and your bowl was taken—hopefully by mistake. You look over at another table and see a bowl, which looks exactly like yours, but it's not yours. You say to yourself, "This one is the same size and looks just like mine, so I'll take this one to replace mine."

---

[20] One who is jealous of another person's possessions

Maybe you've never carried the rationale as far as this little story did, but it's still wrong to take something that doesn't belong to you, and it's still a sin. Watch that your *rationale* does not get in the way of *reason*. We should also watch that we don't talk ourselves into sin. "Oh, it'll be alright. How will someone say that I'm committing a sin?" (Remember, adults are not the only ones watching your actions).

The Cigarette Situation

"I know if I take a puff from just one cigarette, it will be alright because I just want to show them that I can smoke and that I'm cool. That little bit of smoke won't hurt me. I'm around more secondary smoke sometimes, and that hasn't affected me. I don't crave cigarettes. I'm not an addict. I won't get hooked. It's not like I'm doing drugs. I don't do anything else wrong. Nobody will know I took just one little drag. If they ask me again, after this one time, I'll tell them No! I smoked before, and I gave it up. Don't they remember when I quit for last Lent or the time before that when I gave smoking up as my New Year's resolution? I'll just take one little puff. It'll be okay." <u>NOT</u>!!

Who sees what you're doing to your body? Jesus sees and knows. Are our bodies not temples of the Holy Ghost? God cannot dwell in an unclean temple. And if what we do causes our brother to sin, are we not also as guilty as he is? *(Mat. 7:4-5)*

One little puff may lead to a pack, a carton, or an addiction to nicotine or a heavier substance. Secondary smoke is doing more harm than you think it is doing (I have a friend who has *never* smoked, but she has chronic obstructive pulmonary disease [COPD] caused by second-hand smoke because her parents smoked).

Besides the above facts, don't smokers know that you can smell the odor of nicotine[21] in their clothes, in their hair, and on their breath? It's not hidden. Most of the time, people just don't say anything but the odor is very offensive.

Me and Mine

Don't always think, "What's in it for me?" We need to think unselfishly. Helping or giving to someone else often brings rewards that you don't and wouldn't expect. However, if you never give to or help another, how can you expect others to help you when you are in need (physically, mentally, and/or spiritually)? What's in it for you is a reward in heaven that exceeds your wildest dreams here on earth. Give it a try. It won't hurt!

Check In Your Spirit

When we aren't sure what we need to do in a certain situation, it's a tugging of the Holy Ghost at our hearts encouraging us and guiding us. It's a *stop* or a *go* light. If we heed the light, we

---

A colorless, oily, water-soluble, highly toxic, liquid alkaloid, $C_{10}H_{14}N_2$, found in tobacco and valued as an insecticide. ***Lookie**- you're inhaling an insecticide, **WOW!!!**

will avoid pitfalls and dangers when it is red, and, when it is green, we will not miss opportunities that are in our paths.

Question

Why do some people hesitate when you mention *praying* (meditating on God)? All you're doing, when you pray, is *talking directly to God.* He is your best friend. You should never be ashamed or embarrassed to tell or ask Him anything.

Double Time

We're on this earth for two reasons:

1. Maintaining our own personal salvation and
2. Interceding on behalf of and *for* others' Salvation (witnessing to others so they may obtain eternal life).

Truths to Our Beliefs

(*Not misquoted, but a different interpretation by the author*)

The apostles were human beings, and they could have perceived events differently. Only God is infallible.[22] We are to, *"Study to shew thyself approved unto God, a workman that needeth not to be ashamed, rightly dividing the word of truth" (II Tim. 2:15).*

1. How many wise men were there who came to Jesus' birth? There could have been *many* wise men. Just because they presented three gifts to the Christ child doesn't mean that only

[22] Incapable of failing; certain

three men came *(Mat. 2:1)*. Where did the wise men first visit Jesus? Was it in a stable? No! And it wasn't on the same night that He was born *(Mat. 2:11)*.

2. What did Eve eat in the Garden of Eden that she shouldn't have eaten? Well, it wasn't an apple *(Gen 2:17, 3:6).*

3. How many times did the cock crow before Peter denied that he knew Jesus? One time: *(Mat. 26:34)*; two times: *(Mark 14:30)*; one time *(Luke 22:61)*, and one time *(John 18:27)*.

4. How many angels were present at the tomb, during Christ's resurrection? *(Mat. 28:2)* one descended; *(Mark 16:5)* records one man; *(Luke 24:4)* two men; *(John 20:12)* gives an account of two angels.

5. In the "Our Father" *(Mat. 6:9-13; Lk. 11:2-4)*, where is *God's will to be done*? In earth: in us, in our lives. It is to happen right here in and on this planet earth *(Mat. 6:10) (Luke 11:2)*.

6. Was Jesus an only child? *(Mat. 13:55-56)* and *(Mark 6:3)*

Please take a little time, look up the scriptures and learn a little Bible trivia today.

Creating a Blessing

"Honey, that necklace looks so good on you, I wish I had one." Do we tell someone that we like an object that they're wearing in hopes that their charitable Christ-likeness will have them give us that article which we admire? Or are we genuine in our compliments?

Sometimes, if they are led to do so, the unction from the Holy Spirit will have a person give us the shirt off their back. But that usually happens when we don't have an ulterior motive (hidden agendas). Let's not bless others just to receive a blessing in return from them. God will reward us Himself.

Being Kind in All Things

A young woman, wearing a short skirt, walks over to a group of Christian women. One of the women in the group says, "Baby, your knees would look so much better if they were covered up."

The Christian women thought they were being kind in the way they confronted the young lady in the short skirt, but the young lady's feelings were hurt. She was not as knowledgeable, or as strong as the older, more mature ladies who spoke to her from the women's group.

What about another young woman who is sitting in the front row of the church with a short skirt on? Men and women, are on the platform in front of her (yes, even male pastors are vulnerable to the temptation to *look*, and I'm not even going to go into the fact that the young woman may not keep her legs closed and her knees together). What do we do to make an embarrassing situation better? Do we usher her to the rear of the church, or do we (as loving saints) offer this person a lap-cover *ever so inconspicuously*? It's not always *what* you *say* or *do* to a person, but it's *how* you *say* or *do* something, that really matters. *"...with loving kindness have I drawn thee" (Jer. 31:3c).*

The Monument

I've heard it said, "Lord, tear down or destroy this mountain" (that thing which disturbs the natural flow of your life). **No**! The Word says to pray that the mountains in your life be moved (remove – to take away, withdraw, or eliminate). By moving the mountain, it will remain in existence as a testimony of *that which was* in your way. Even though it still stands somewhere else, it does not stand in your path. The word remove denotes that an object or situation is going to be somewhere else after it has been moved *(Mat. 17:20, 21:21)*. Let those mountains in your lives be a *testament* of the *tests* you've overcame.

Hold On — Be Strong

"Submit yourself therefore to God. Resist the devil, and he will flee from you" (James. 4:7). Make sure you're strong enough to resist. You should be strong in your faith and in God's Word. *"Finally, my brethren, be strong in the Lord, and in the power of his might" (Eph. 6:10)*. We must know the Bible in order to be resistant. *"Study to shew thyself approved unto God, a workman that needeth not to be ashamed, rightly dividing the word of truth" (II Tim. 2:15)*. If you take the time to listen to Him, the Lord will teach you.

Order

It is ours to command, but *order* belongs to God. Not *our* will, but *His Will* is to be done. *"Let all things be done decently and in order" (I Cor. 14:40).*

Santa Claus

> The true story of Santa Claus begins with Nicholas, who was born during the third century in the village of Patara. At the time the area was Greek and is now on the southern coast of Turkey. His wealthy parents, who raised him to be a devout Christian, died in an epidemic while Nicholas was still young. Obeying Jesus' words to "sell what you own and give the money to the poor," Nicholas used his whole inheritance to assist the needy, the sick, and the suffering. He dedicated his life to serving God and was made Bishop of Myra while still a young man. Bishop Nicholas became known throughout the land for his generosity to those in need, his love for children, and his concern for sailors and ships.[23]

Americans have chosen a jolly old fictitious man dressed in a red and white suit to represent Saint Nicholas or Santa Claus. The world has adopted this man to represent hope, love, joy, peace, goodness, gentleness, and faith, not realizing that the hope that they search for is in the fruit of God's Holy Spirit.

Parents have told their children falsehoods about this man, who supposedly comes down the chimney bearing gifts, and then more lies to cover up the fact that there is no chimney in their house or apartment. We shouldn't lie, especially to our children. This

---

[23] St. Nicholas Center, www.stnicholascenter.org, Holland, Michigan.

myth has caused us to mound one lie on top of another. Children should know the truth about Santa Claus (he *was* a good man), the tooth fairy, the Easter bunny, monsters in the closet and under the bed; they don't exist, period!

Man

"What is man, that thou art mindful of him? and the son of man, that thou visitest him? For thou hast made him a little lower than the angels, and hast crowned him with glory and honour" (Ps. 8:4-5).

What is he? He is a spirit being; He has a soul (mind, will, and emotions), and he lives in a body. That's man. The body is a *temporary* shell, a casing to house the fundamental elements of man's being. Man's soul houses the imagination, reason, memory, and the affections.

The most important part of Man's make-up is his Spirit. It's man's 'Conscience', 'Communion with God', 'Intuition', 'Faith', 'Hope', 'Reverence', 'Prayer' and 'Worship' all directed to God and Him alone. The Spirit is the immortal part of a human being. To know a person by their "Spirit Man" is to know them without the interaction of their mind or the body, yet sometimes when we talk about man's Soul and his Spirit, they are used simultaneously (at the same time). It has been said that a man's eyes are the windows to his soul. Sometimes we can look into a person's eyes and know that person by his *Spirit Man*. We sense an association with the other person; it's a sense of knowing that person.

Some people may call our Spirit Man "Karma"[24] Karma is not part of a Christians' make-up. The soul of a man can get him into trouble. We should never allow our feelings to take control of us. We need to take control of what we say, what we do and how we think. We should be guided by our Spirit Man, who is the controller of our *triune* being (spirit, soul & body).

Sometimes when we want to 'Bless' someone (act of kindness), all three of our 'beings' have to work together in order for that act to take place. Our *Soul* has to receive the desire to help. Our *Spirit* has to express the 'love' that it took to enforce that desire. And now our *Body* (the physical being) must deliver that act of kindness. In other words, "I would enjoy taking Aunt Millie shopping and she probably would appreciate it too." It's the Spirit, Soul & Body working together for a demonstration of the Complete Man.

"But as it is written, Eye hath not seen, nor ear heard, neither have entered into the heart of man, the things which God hath prepared for them that love him. But God hath revealed them unto us by his Spirit: for the Spirit searcheth all things, yea, the deep things of God. For what man knoweth the things of a man, save the spirit of man which is in him? even so the things of God knoweth no man, but the Spirit of God." I Cor. 2:9-11

---

[24] (*Hinduism, Buddhism*. action, seen as bringing upon oneself inevitable results, good or bad, either in this life or in a reincarnation. [This is another subject that we must deal with in another book – please remind me when you see me.])

Are You A Player, Or A Spectator?

Player:

Active Participant — Paid a specific amount per game

Crosses the goal line — Plays in the game

Spectator:

Watches from the sidelines — Watches touchdowns being made

Paid according to his workload

Passive Participant (just sits around waiting for something to happen)

"But be ye <u>*doers*</u> *of the Word, and not hearers only, deceiving your own selves" (James 1:22).* You've got to be a *team player* when you sign up to be on the Lord's team, if you want to carry the ball. If God desires you to witness (tell of the Good News) to someone, you've got to be a willing and yielding vessel. You've got to *go* and *do* whatever *it* may be. *Ecclesiastes 9:10* also points out that we should do that which our Father would have for us to do. *"Whatsoever thy hand findeth to do, do it with thy might; for there is no work, nor device, nor knowledge, nor wisdom, in the grave, whither thou goest."* (If that one was too rough for you, you may want to read another translation, but it's still the Bible anyway you read it).

Tried and True

We will be *tried* (tested and proved good, dependable, and trustworthy) here on earth, but it is to *refine* (to become more fine, elegant, or polished) us for the kingdom of God. The process must be done in order that we may be worthy ambassadors for God and be in right standing with man. *Faith* in God's Word is a key element to the process, and prayer is necessary to strengthen that faith.

We need the Sword of the Spirit (Bible) to strengthen our defenses. There are people out there (false prophets) who know the Word, and they'll use the Bible to get what they want and to deceive, mislead, misguide, misdirect, misinform, and separate us from the love of God and each other in the fellowship of the church.

"For I am persuaded, that neither death, nor life, nor angels, nor principalities, nor powers, nor things present, nor things to come, Nor height, nor depth, nor any other creature, shall be able to separate us from the love of God, which is in Christ Jesus our Lord." Rom 8:38-39

Temptation

We are *tempted* of the devil, yet we are *proven and tried* by God. We sometimes go through *trials*, *tribulations* and *trying times*, yet these instances help to mold and refine us. People may *try* to *test* us, yet we can be assured that *Immanuel* is with us.

Look at Job, the three Hebrew boys, Daniel, and yes, even Jesus. If we look at any of their situations, we see that in the end, their tribulations gave way to comfort in the protective arms of God. We're never alone as long as we keep God first and foremost in our lives. He knows that we will come out as pure gold because He cares for us *(I Cor. 10:13)*, (*James 1:12*), and (*I Pet. 1:6-7* and *4:12*. Check out His Word.

"Blessed be God, even the Father of our Lord Jesus Christ, the Father of mercies, and the God of all comfort; Who comforteth us in all our tribulation, that we may be able to comfort them which are in any trouble, by the comfort wherewith we ourselves are comforted of God. For as the sufferings of Christ abound in us, so our consolation also aboundeth by Christ. And whether we be afflicted, it is for your consolation and salvation, which is effectual in the enduring of the same sufferings which we also suffer: or whether we be comforted, it is for your consolation and salvation. And our hope of you is stedfast, knowing, that as ye are partakers of the sufferings, so shall ye be also of the consolation." (II Cor. 1:3-7)

A Poem

"Little trials may come your way, but be encouraged."

"They may rock and roll your day, but be encouraged."[25]

Life Is Not A Soap Opera

Though the Storms are raging in you life *("Secret Storms")*; there is a *"Guiding Light"* whose name is ***Jesus***. You only have *"One Life to Live"* in this present world. Now is the time to get your house in order. There may not be time to *"Search For Tomorrow"*. We are in the last *"Days of Our Lives"*. *"As The World Turns"*, life should be lived in Christ. *"Jesus answered, "I am the way and the truth and the life. No one comes to the Father except through me" John 14:6.*

(Sorry if a 'soap' that you know about was not mentioned. It wasn't necessary for this short story and it is <u>not</u> meant to glorify them. Please, put your rocks down & change the channel ;)

---

[25] Quote from V. Poller

To View or Not To View — No Question

During a home visitation with an older Christian Woman, who was watching soap operas, a thought occurred to me. If the soap, which we as Christians shouldn't be cluttering our minds with anyway, can't be turned off while the person visiting you is in your home, and you can't direct your attention to that which is at hand (someone who really cares about you and is there to offer you assistance, company, prayer, and some Good News), then the person visiting you shouldn't stay and waste their time. That behavior (watching TV with visitors around) is rude!

Soaps, in general, are depressing. They deal with someone having an affair, or who is having issues. They are formulated to make you go off to a land where you don't have to face the same types of issues that may be going on in your life. The people on the TV are actors. They have a script, directors, and everyone in production knows the outcome of the storyline. What the writers came up with may not solve your similar situation. As I said before, "Only Jesus can solve it."

Watch out for those one hour talk shows, too. Some are informative, while others are just ***smut***.

Hearing God

I enjoy hearing a word from God through others who hear His voice when our Father speaks. Other people's messages frequently assure me that I'm following the straight and narrow path of righteousness. It is wonderful to receive a confirmation from God through others. *"Because straight is the gate, and narrow is the way, which leadeth unto life, and few there be that find it" (Mat. 7:14).*

Why Do Christians Gather Together?

We gather together to worship and fellowship with God, to hear and get an understanding of what He has to say from His Word, because He commanded us to enjoy fellowshipping one with another. *"Not forsaking the assembling of ourselves together, as the manner of some is; but exhorting one another: and so much the more, as ye see the day approaching" (Heb. 10:25).* To be better equipped to go about our Father's business (i.e., winning people for the kingdom of God and sharing the good news of how to prosper while on this planet). And we gather together to learn what we must do to make it in this world we live in.

As we delight ourselves in the Word of God, time and time again, we discover yet another blessing which we might previously have overlooked. You can read a passage of scripture, and some things don't become clear until someone else says it.

God is our creator and protector. It's at times of distress, persecution, despair, loneliness, and trouble that we need to be around other Christians who are strong in the faith. We should also be there spiritually, emotionally and sometimes physically for one another when we're needed.

When you're surrounded by worldly people, and they know that you're a child of God, these various people may sometimes treat you differently. Some may respect you, while others will try to *test* you to see what you'll say or do. Something may be said or done around you that isn't right, and the world, knowing you to be a Christian, will look to see what your reaction will be. Temptation to fall into a trap of sin will still be around, but we don't have to fall into the trap. A dirty joke may be told in your presence and the world wants to see if you'll go along with it. Christians are continually under a microscope to *prove* whom we intend to follow: God or the devil.

We gather together to love, learn, and laugh together. Yes, we Christians can laugh and have a good time while we're here on earth. The world sees us as being serious (hell and damnation), but we can have a good time in the Lord while we minister for our God and His kingdom. Being saved isn't boring.

Speak To Me Lord

God is *subtle* (faint or delicate in quality) when He speaks. We must be still sometimes to hear Him, if not, we miss His voice. God may speak to us in an *audible* voice, but most of the time, He speaks in a *whisper* to our heart. All we have to do is listen.

Rescue 9-1-1

The television program "Rescue 9-1-1" had a story line of amazing things that happened to people as reported by an emergency medical team. The show could also have been called, "Miracle in the Works." Cardio Pulmonary Resuscitation (CPR) is a miracle in itself. We actually breathe life back into a person by the divine will of God.

More on "Rescue 9-1-1"

When a person drowns and is without oxygen for a long period of time, and that same person is brought back to consciousness without any signs of permanent brain damage, then that's a "Miracle 9-1-1."

When a small child falls to the concrete pavement from the third floor level of a building, and that child's Pamper® explodes on impact, while the child has no broken bones or internal injuries, then that's a "Miracle 9-1-1."

Give It Up – Turn It Loose – Let It Alone!

When we become new creatures in Christ (born again or saved), we have to give up that *old* man, those *old* habits and learn to start anew. The devil is a master of disguises, and we must see him for who he really is. Our spiritual eyes give us a so-called X-ray vision. The devil has many special delivery packages for us: trouble, war, grief, sickness, woes, sadness, depression, and backbiting to name a few. **Christ** is offering **Eternal Life** through His uncut, unadulterated Word (the Bible). Jesus Christ offers **Hope,** and He has *NO* disguises.

Manifestations

Have you noticed that most of those persons who *were* healed in the Old and New Testaments asked to be healed, and they also *believed* that they would be healed *("Beloved, I wish above all things that thou mayest prosper and be in health, even as thy soul prospereth" III John 2)*?

"Centurion Servant"	Luke 7:1-7
"Two Blind Men"	Mat. 20:30-34
"Man with an Unclean Spirit"	Mark 1:23-26
"Man Sick of the Palsy"	Mark 2:3-5, 12
"Jarius' Daughter"	Mark 5:22-42
(Two miracles at once)	
"Woman with an Issue of Blood"	Mark 5:25-34

When we don't see the manifestation of a healing, it may be because of our own *disbelief*, or the healing was not in the *realm of God's perfect plan* at that time *("When Jesus heard that, he said, This sickness is not unto death, but for the glory of God, that the Son of God might be glorified thereby" John 11:4)*. A lot of times when a person prays, they don't see or feel results right away, so they give up and give in to the enemy. The devil *does not want* us to be well.

The ministers, who lay hands on the afflicted individual, count the healing to be done according to God's will. We ministers are satisfied; we know God has done that which He has promised. We're done with it.

It's time for people to put faith into action *("And when he had called unto him his twelve disciples, he gave them power against unclean spirits, to cast them out, and to heal all manner of sickness and all manner of disease" Mat. 10:1)* or don't bother to ask, believe, and receive. To receive a healing, a person has to speak those things into existence and believe God. *("For verily I say unto you, That whosoever shall say unto this mountain, Be thou removed, and be thou cast into the sea; and shall not doubt in his heart, but shall believe that those things which he saith shall come to pass; he shall have whatsoever he saith" Mark 11:23).*

Has God ever *not* granted one of your prayer requests? Could it have been that the request may not have been according to His will, or the time for us to receive that blessing had not yet come to pass, or because we asked amiss? *("Ye ask, and receive not, because ye ask amiss, that ye may consume it upon your lusts" James 4:3).*

If we are stricken with a debilitating illness—one that keeps us in bondage—instead of feeling sorry for ourselves, why don't we seek ways to give God the glory until our healing can manifest itself? We must look to magnify the Lord for His greatness in spite of our difficulties and afflictions.

Miracle Manifestation

I've experienced many miracles in my short lifetime. One must be careful sometimes about our telling of such wonders of the Lord. No, it's not luck as some people may call it; miracles are blessings from God.

Some people get discouraged and upset that God has not done a miracle for them, and they get mad at God.

Once I was coming out of a store, and it was pouring rain. I had no umbrella with me, and the Lord knew that I had just done my hair that morning. Don't you know, He stopped the rain long enough for me to get into my car, and then He sent the rain pouring down again? Now, some people may not consider that to be a miracle, or that it was no big deal, but it was a big thing for me. I *believe* He did it for me. Don't you know He'll do a similar thing for you too? Just *believe* and *recognize*!

Called by God or Man?

Are we walking a tightrope? Are we giving *God* or *man* the glory? "God gave me the Gift of Discernment;" or "Sister Sookie told me that she got a Word from God that I was supposed to be a pastor of a mega church around the corner from …" Man-made or God ordained? Are we fulfilling the prophesy that is within us? That prophesy which God has established, or are we trying to live up to someone else's prophesy[26] to us? Make sure you're hearing from God before you go *stepping out* into a *calling* (pastor, teacher, prophet, etc.) or a *ministry.*

Who Do You Trust?

Did you know that the devil doesn't want you or me in part? He's aiming for 100%. Some people believe: "The devil doesn't

---

[26] to declare or foretell by or as if by divine inspiration

want me. If I leave him alone, then he'll leave me alone." Not true! He wants 100% of all he can get, and then he'll throw you to the side until he's ready to use you again for his evil deeds. Yes, if you allow him to, the devil *does* desire to use you.

God also wants us to share with Him an everlasting happiness in heaven and an abundant life while here on earth. But God, too, wants 100% of you. He's waiting to give you the best. Now my question to you is: "Who are *you* going to trust?"

Picture This

Situation: there's a football lying on the ground with a group of players standing around looking at it, and the conversation heard goes something like this:

"Guess we're gonna make a touch-down soon." "I wonder how far I could run with that ball." "I never played football before; I'll look silly." "Someone else will pick up the ball and run with it. I'll wait until they do." "I'm not running. I'll mess up my hair. Don't you run either." "Oh! I was gonna take it, but I'll let the quarterback score the goal." "I'm too tired, and I did enough already." "I'd play, but I don't have the right uniform (what happened to come as you are?)" What excuses are these people trying to make?

Now take a look at *your* position that you hold within *your* church. Aren't we supposed to *help* the church and others? Is someone losing the game because they aren't taking an active part as a team player.

We must seek to ask God where we fit in and where He would have us to serve. Be encouraged! *(I Cor.9: 24-25, II Tim. 4:7, Phil. 3:14 & Mat. 13:12, 25:29).* Did you grab your Bible? Go get it and read those scriptures. *Please*. Let's get Busy!

Quit Skating and Start Working

The Church *needs* to get rid of its ***Spiritual Crutches***.

Too many people are allowing other members to do all the work around the church and community, while those persons who are not working reap all the benefits. These *spiritual freeloaders* see things being accomplished around the physical church structure, and they say to themselves, "It's getting done (whatever *it* may be), and they don't need me to help." Wrong answer! It takes more than one person to sweep a floor, pick up pieces of paper, or see a need and meet that need. You don't have to have a special anointing, a certain gift, a specific title, or a position within the church to help out. It *should* be a desire within you. If you don't have the desire to help, pray for it and cultivate your faith so that the work within your spirit will surface to the physical man.

Wishing and Waiting

Don't sit around and expect *it* to happen. If you can, *help* to make it happen and remember that God has given us control.

If I want a job, I must look for one, fill out an application, and expect an interview while continually thanking God all the way. The same goes for the church—if you really want to help, you must apply yourself, ask what you can do, and then do it!

Ushers

"I'd rather be a door keeper in the house of my God. Then dwell in the tents of wickedness" (Ps. 84:10).

Picture This:

Doorkeeper—standing at the door in the house of God: You are in God's house serving our Lord by being on duty at your post. You protect that which is inside the building. You intercede with prayer on behalf of others. You are there at your post to serve and to take care of the household of faith.

Sometimes it can be a thankless duty, yet, if the usher is sincere and faithful in what he (or she) does to serve, his reward will be in heaven. Also thank God for those people who sometimes *will* give a nod, a smile, or a thank you for all that you do.

No! It does not mean you are traveling down the path of wickedness if you are not an usher. It will not put you in a higher position in heaven, nor put you in a lower tax bracket if you do become an usher.

The church needs more people who are willing to offer themselves in dedication, commitment, and availability. If this is not your calling, please pray that more laborers are called and that they accept this responsibility with joy.

The Lord's Prayer

Why do some people want to call it other than the Lord's Prayer? Some people want to call it "The Disciple's Prayer." Yes, the disciples did ask Jesus to teach them to pray, and yes, we—as disciples of Christ—say the prayer, but wasn't it the Lord, who was inspired to pray to the Father? Who said the prayer? Why rename something that is known and recognized by so many people? It's like renaming a pumpkin and calling it a *large orange squash.* People ask for a pumpkin when that's what they really want. They don't know *your* new name for it.

Where's the Rock?

After God created the earth, have you ever thought about where the *sand ends* and where the *earth* (dirt) begins? If you go to a beach there is nothing but sand. As you move closer inland, the sand usually mingles with soil, and there you will begin to find growths of grass, trees, foliage and all sorts of greenery.

Has man built some houses on sand instead of laying a solid foundation of God's Word on the firmer soil mixed with rocks? Jesus is the solid rock. Build upon His Word. *"The LORD liveth; and blessed be my rock; and let the God of my salvation be exalted" (Ps. 18:46).*

Getting Even

Even though some people may act like idiots, you still must not get nasty, act rude, or get even with them. You've heard the sayings: "Two wrongs don't make a right," or "You can catch more flies with honey than you can with vinegar." It's true. Try it and see for yourself.

Deceptive Production

"A tree is known by the fruit it bears." You've got to watch out for deceitful, dishonest or misleading *fruit*.

When you see the fruit of an *Orange Tree*, the fruit is green in color at first, and then it turns yellow, and then orange. After awhile, you may think that you have *limes* and later *lemons*. When you wait until the fruit is mature, you will see that it is an *orange tree* by the final stage of the fully-ripened crop.

So too, must we examine the *Spirit* by the *Word of God*. A person can quote scriptures and tell you chapter and verse, but is that person bearing mature fruit in his or her witness? You have to know the Bible for yourself. You've also got to check and see if he or she is being a *doer* of God's Word too. "*But be ye doers of the word, and not hearers only, deceiving your own selves*" (*James 1:22*).

It's All Right; Not!

Our nation is in trouble when our society applauds or lets adultery, fornication, and infidelity *slide-by* through the media. It's not just exploited on talk shows, but in movies, books, on radio, in music, and etc. You don't have to listen, watch, or talk about negatives or demeaning topics. Keep it pure.

It's In There

All of the stories in the Bible are *situations*, with a God-given *solution.* Got a problem? Get the book! You've got this one; now pick up your Bible.

Ain't Too Proud

Could we get a healing the same way that some of the people in the New Testament did? It may have been a little gross, but it got the job done.

Mark 8:22-23: Jesus spit on the blind man's eyes.

Mark 10:46-52: Jesus healed blind Bartimaeus by telling him to *go his way*, (in other words—take a walk). Now that's faith with a capital "F!"

Mat. 20:29-34: Two blind men, sitting by the wayside, and all it took was *just a touch.* Wow!

John 9:11: Jesus spit on the ground and made clay. Would we be too sophisticated to have Jesus spit on us today? (But don't go around spitting on people; God will give you another alternative.) If we have faith as a grain of mustard seed, we can have it all. Trust – Believe – Receive!

Do Not Disturb!!!

If you are running late for a service, and you are part of the leadership (or even a member), don't create a scene by coming to the front of the auditorium, shaking hands, and throwing out a greeting on the way up to the front, and disturbing the meeting/service or class. It's rude to God and to the speaker who may be talking. If your place is in the front, then God will make a way for you. To avoid all this drama, *be on time* or even be a little early for *consecrated prayer time.*

Wow!!

Don't *Vegetate*, just *Anticipate*. *Expect* the *unexpected.*

Know Who You're Calling

God's number is ***not*** 1-900-PSYCHIC. We have a direct line to our Father through PRA-YERS. His line is *never* busy, and He won't hang up on you or put you on hold. He's always available and the bill was paid for by your brother, Jesus Christ. God is only a prayer away. Jesus or God (we'll get to the Blessed Trinity later) is on the main line. Call Him collect and He *will* accept the charges.

Bad Habits

One way to get away from a bad habit is to *fast.*[27] Whatever negative thing it may be, give it up to the Lord for one week. Pray

---

[27] an abstinence from food, or a limiting of one's food. Abstain, keep away from, or give up something.

and devote time to God and see what happens. Ask your pastor to give you instructions on *Fasting*.

Sin, Suicide and Such

When a person takes their own life, are they playing "Russian Roulette" with God? This is written so *you* do not consider this alternative action as a way out from frustrations, difficulties, trials, disappointment, or depression.

Okay, someone takes their life by shooting himself or herself and they die. If Jesus were to come back at that very moment, what would be that person's outcome? If they did not have a chance to ask God to forgive them for what they did, where would they be spending eternity? Our prayer is that they did have the opportunity to make things right with God. It's chancy. Would we want to take a chance of the sinful act of suicide being the gun, and the hour of Christ's return being that one bullet ready to fire from the gun's chamber? Don't take that chance.

If you know of someone who has committed suicide, always offer up much prayer for the family and friends who remain behind. Strength, hope, understanding, and love are the offertory prayers and consolation that friends and families need in times like those.

Don't use suicide as your only way out. There ***is*** hope and that hope is in Jesus Christ.

Good Girls

There was a time when men would hustle to a church seeking a good, righteous, church-going woman. Where have those times gone?

The Gift

It wasn't given to you on Christmas, because we don't wait to express ourselves on just one day and besides that, it's Jesus' birthday and not yours.

It wasn't given on Valentine's Day because we love you all year long.

It wasn't given on St. Patrick's Day, because we, as Christians, don't believe in luck.

It wasn't given on your birthday because we're glad that God had a purpose just for you on that day—you were born, and that was special enough.

It was given because of the love that God instills in us to be obedient when He calls us to bestow blessings on someone, and to give that gift whenever He asks us to bless someone.

Just Do It!

The phrase, "Just do it" appears on almost everything from clothing, to books, to signs, and etc. My question is: **"Just do what?"** Do we do what makes us feel good (i.e., drink until we pass out and don't remember where we've been)? Do we do what we want to do? "Just do it," even if it's wrong (i.e., rob a bank or lie to save face)? "Just do it" with no regards for the other guy (i.e., cheat a person out of what's rightfully theirs)? Does it mean don't think about it (i.e., "It's not any of my business, so I don't care"). "*Just do it*?" Again, we've got to consider the consequences of our actions before we "Just do it."

Dress

If we have to pull on it or keep adjusting it (a dress, skirt or top), then it may not be proper to wear. Think about it. It may be too tight (get something less tight), too loose (take it in), or too short or too revealing. Would God want His children to wear clothes that are unbecoming? If a person cannot afford new, then they should seek out consignment or gently-used clothing stores for more affordable attire. I do.

Regarding Love

We continue to have *love* for a person who lives in sin, yet we may have *dislike* of the actions taking place in that persons' life—homosexuality, drug abuse, murder, robbery, and the like.

Prayer is needed to divide the two emotions. We have to keep the *dislike* out of our spirit and keep the *love* of Jesus in our hearts for that person who may be trapped in sin.

The Apostles Creed

I believe in God, the Father Almighty Creator of heaven and earth *(Is. 40:28)* and in Jesus Christ, His only Son our Lord; Who was conceived by the Holy Ghost, born of the Virgin Mary *(Mat. 1:18-25)*, suffered under Pontius Pilate *(Mat. 27:1-26)* was crucified, died, and was buried *(Mark 15)*. He descended into Hell *(Rev. 1:18)*; the third day He arose again *(I Cor. 15:4)* from the dead *(Acts 10:40)*; He ascended into heaven *(John 20:17)*, sitteth at the right hand of God *(I Pet. 3:22)*, the Father Almighty *(Mat. 26:64, Acts 2:33)*; from thence He shall come to judge the living and the dead *(Acts 10:42, II Tim. 4:1)*. I believe in the Holy Ghost *(I Cor. 12:1-11, John 14:26)*, the holy church *(Mat. 16:18)*, the communion of saints *(Heb. 10:25, II Cor. 8:4)*, the forgiveness of sins *(Col. 1:14, James 5:15)*, the resurrection of the body and life everlasting *(John 11:24-27, Heb. 6:2)*. Amen.

Who Are You Trying To Convince?

If we are plain in appearance (hair undone, or you need some; breath—not fresh—gotta get a TicTac™), how can we convince the *unsaved* into being a part of a *sanctified lifestyle*? What do we, as Christians, have to offer on the surface compared to what the world has to offer?

When I was much younger, there were women who wore long black dresses, un-straightened hair wrapped in a hairnet under a black pill box hat, what I called “old-lady shoes,” and, to top it off, black cotton stockings. I would cross the street to get away from these women with their tracts (little pamphlets talking about churchy things). If I had to look like them, I didn't want to be a part of anything they represented. Before we can minister to a person's spirit man and introduce them to Christ, we must first get our foot in the doorway (their eyes).

We need to dress according to the locale where we are ministering and have good hygiene (be clean). If you wear make-up and perfume, put some on. If you do need more hair, go out and buy some. If you need to enhance your outer beauty (some extensions [no, I didn't say whether they should be hair or nails]), by all means, please do so.

Wise Men

The wise men were *Astrologers*. In the time before Christ was born, men were needed to make maps and were guided by the direction of the stars for night travel.

Today, man has added superstition and mysticism to an old form of map-making. Psychics are not wise men. God gives men visions as He sees fit, but it is to God that glory is to be given and not to any man.

"Hey Mon, You Got The Time?"

"What time is church over?" Answer: Whenever God *wants* or *allows* His *guests* to go home or leave His presence. *"Quench not the Spirit"* (*I Thess. 5:19*).

Would you rush out of someone's home after you've been invited for dinner? I hope not. You would stay and have some conversation, dessert, and relax a little while. So too, when we come into the house of the Lord (the church), we need to *sit a spell* and relax. Enjoy His presence.

Incest

Incest—sexual intercourse between closely related persons

It is immoral, but why isn't it against man's law? Would you believe that it *is* against man's law; however, there are still people who will attempt to get away with this perversion of incest and people who will turn a blind eye to it?

License

Only two times in the Bible is the word *licence* used: first in *Acts 21:40*, and then in *Acts 25:16*. The meaning of licence in the first scripture means to give leave, to permit. In the second scripture it means location, condition or opportunity. There is no mention of License[28] *at all* in the Word of God. A piece of paper does not give you the spiritual right to preach or teach God's Word.

Jesus commissioned His disciples to do a work for the Father. No papers were signed or exchanged. God calls and man acknowledges that calling. He could call you to be an apostle, a teacher, a healer, a helper, or He may place you wherever He needs

---

[28] formal permission from a governmental or other constituted authority to do something, as to carry on some business or profession

your service *"And he gave some, apostles; and some, prophets; and some, evangelists; and some, pastors and teachers; For the perfecting of the saints, for the work of the ministry, for the edifying of the body of Christ." Eph. 4:11-12*

It is man who makes that calling different and sometimes difficult by not knowing if we hear from ourselves or from God. Both Christian man and worldly man have contributed to this confusion. Know that you are called of God, and then step out in faith.

I'm Only Kidding

As Christians, we should not play *practical jokes*. All that jokes are is a lie. Watch those lies on "April Fool's Day" too. Making a fool of someone may cause hurts that you cannot imagine or may ever know.

Right Here and Now

No, the planet earth is not our real home,[29] nor are we in heaven, but we can be blessed while we're on earth. We know that every good and perfect gift comes from God *(James 1:17)*. As we continue to strive towards better things, He restores our souls, while making our pastures green *(Ps. 23)*. We can reap the benefits that God has promised us through His Word right here *(Gal. 6:9)*. When we follow God's Word, we unlock the door to His blessings. When we walk and talk using our faith *("For we walk by faith, not by sight" II Cor. 5:7),* we capture His attention. We're to think positive thoughts

---

[29] See *This is Not My Home (pg 100)*

(*true, honest, just, pure, lovely, and of good report, if there contains any virtue or any praise; then we're to think on that kind of stuff. Phil. 4:8*).

God does inhabit the praise of His people *("But thou are holy, O thou that inhabitest the praises of Israel" Ps. 22:3),* who are called by His name *(II Ch.7:14)*. If we trust in Him with all our heart *(Prov. 3:5)*, then our dreams will come true *(Ps. 37:5).* We must strive towards the *sanctified best*, while we enjoy our lives on earth, before we seek to make heaven our home.

This Is Not My Home
(John 8:23)

> *"Because of the sin of Adam, you were sent to earth; so that I, the Lord, would know whom to share my kingdom with. You will weed yourselves out and I will know who is for me or against me. You make the choice. You follow the rules and regulations (The Bible) yourself. Don't cheat off of your neighbor; he may have the wrong answers".*[30]

We are given a **map** (the Bible) to get home (heaven). If we follow it, we will reach our destination; if not, we will be lost on another road (destruction).

We get signals from other bases (religions, sects, denominations) but are the signals from our home base? Let us press toward the mark for the prize, which is in Christ Jesus.

---

[30] Inspirational word given to V. Poller by the Holy Spirit

While we are on this earth, we have a purpose, a goal. We have work to complete before returning to our home base. We must make our quota before returning home (salvation for lost souls). We are to inform (witness to) and seek out those who desire a better place when we leave this world. We must let them know they have a choice: to return home (heaven) to be happy (an eternal R & R)[31], or forever burn in hell. We're on temporary duty (TDY) at this present time on earth. We're going to have a permanent change of station (PCS) when we relocate to the third heaven.

We are here on earth to sell a product (Salvation). Packaging of our product must be right. What we say, how we look and how we act are of the utmost importance.

Advertising must be appealing. "No more hatred, no more sin, no more war …only the best." We must be able to communicate the word of God. We are not of this world, but we've got to fit in. *Clothes* should be modest, yet timely; *speech,* clear and understandable, yet powerful; and *mannerisms* should be kind and walking tall in the love and truth of our Lord and Savior, Jesus Christ.

We are equipped with tools to aid us on our way: **Prayer** is our direct line to headquarters (secret weapon). The **Holy Spirit:** He is a charged beeper, just like the commercial for E. F. Hutton: when

[31] Rest and Relaxation

God speaks, we stop everything to listen, and we must have ears to hear. "Let's hear a word from ***our*** sponsor."

The following are helping tools we will use to assist us to get home. **The Holy Bible:** our map and compass. **A Prime Example:** the life of Jesus. **Praise and worship:** a ladder to and from heaven. **Saints of God:** give encouragement. **Fellowship:** our booster shots.

Finally, when physical death occurs, and our mission on earth is finished, we can say, "It is well; beam me up, Jesus." Will you be ready when He calls?

Ask and Receive

It's easy to ask God for a blessing, but why is it so hard to

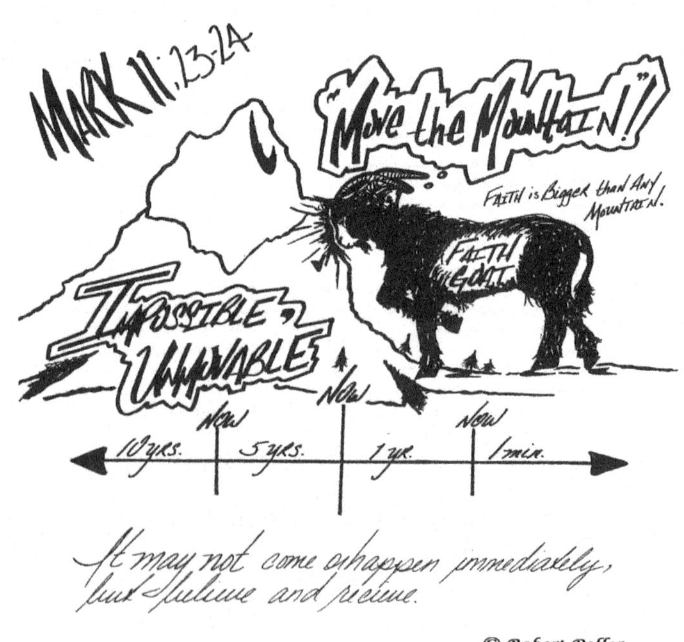

ask Him for forgiveness of a sin? Asking Him for forgiveness should be as easy as asking for a cheeseburger at a café, only - without the wait.

Asking and Receiving

When we ask God for something, what do we do next? Do we sit, wait, hope, and expect God to zap it up for us? Or do we just take one step, knowing that God will take two, while we trust God to give us the desires of our heart according to His word? *("Delight thyself also in the LORD: and he shall give thee the desires of thine heart." Ps. 37:4).*

We have to do some *leg work* and investigate the possibilities. Is our desire obtainable and within our means? Is our desire being gluttonous? Yes, we are to desire that of royalty, yet within realistic limits. Don't crave a diamond ring and a Rolls Royce when there's no food on the table and the electric and gas bills are due.

Go to God in prayer and *ask* Him for whatever is needed, and do it with a pure heart (*just one time*). Sure, sometimes we want to confirm with ourselves that God has heard our plea, so we beg God over and over again to grant our requests. Nevertheless, as parents hear their child's petitions, dad or mom may not always respond at just that very moment. Sometimes it's not the proper time for us to ask. Then again, parents might have heard their child's request and have chosen not to answer at that time; the same goes with our asking Father God for anything. We don't have to nag God, but just *ask, believe,* and *then receive*.

There is a difference between our *giving a request over to God,* and *our trying to help God to make things happen for us* (creating our own blessing). We must see what the Bible has to say about our particular supplication and, by all means, keep the faith.

Sometimes God will place someone on your heart. You imagine seeing their face, or something material like a trinket or a picture might remind you of that person. There are times when we need to intercede (pray) for a friend, relative, or an acquaintance. We may not know why; however, God knows. It's our responsibility to yield to the unction of the Holy Spirit and trust Him.

To Be, Or Not To Be—Selfish

The Lord may be trying to show us how some requests that people are making, are not being answered. Are we asking God for something because we *want* it, *just* like we want it, *right* here and *right* now? Father God is like any other Father; He loves us and wants to bestow blessings upon us. *"Delight thyself also in the LORD: and he shall give thee the desires of thine heart" (Ps. 37:4).*

Do we try to second guess God by saying, "I want to own a particular house, by a particular date, on a particular street"? Sure God said to be specific about what we want when we pray *("Therefore*

I say unto you, what things soever ye desire, when ye pray, believe that ye receive them, and ye shall have them" Mark 11:24), but are we allowing God to be God in our lives, or are we trying to box God into a corner, by trying to get Him to consent to our wishes?

Are we asking to be a *blessing to others*, or are we being selfish in what we're asking God for? *("Ye lust, and have not: ye kill, and desire to have, and cannot obtain: ye fight and war, yet ye have not, because ye ask not. Ye ask, and receive not, because ye ask amiss, that ye may consume it upon your lusts" James 4:2-3).* We have to ask ourselves: "Are our motives right in what we want?"

Could it be that we are demanding that things be done our way, even in Jesus name, when we should be saying, "Not my will, but Thy will be done?" *("Saying, Father, if thou be willing, remove this cup from me: nevertheless not my will, but thine, be done" Luke 22:42).* Are we trying to confuse boldness with brazenness? Maybe we're not asking God if it is His will, but instead, we brazenly let Him know that *our* wills must be met. Is this the answer to the question regarding why we are not hearing from God?

We must *ask*, *believe*, and then be ready to *receive*. *Anyone* can follow a crowd, but it takes *someone special* to lead others in the *right* direction. Dare to be different. Be *you*, yet be unique. Let's share God's Word through our examples.

God Told Me To, Didn't He?

A prophet comes to town and tells you that you are going to be the first woman preacher in this area. It sounds good, and you wouldn't mind preaching, but just because something was prophesied to happen in our life does not mean that we or someone else has to be a catalyst (helper) for these things coming to pass. God said that our gifts would make room for us: *"A man's gift maketh room for him, and bringeth him before great men" (Prov. 18:16)*, and we don't have to help God out.

You've Got To Earn It

When the children of Israel left Egypt, God did not say, "***Shazamn"*** and *poof!* There they were in the Promised Land. No, the children of God had to *achieve* the land, and, after awhile, God saw that they were finally *worthy*.

So too must we, as children of God, be worthy of what God has in store for us. We must aim to achieve all of that which God has promised to us in the Bible. Are you being worthy of God's best?

Tell Somebody

"Let Your Request be made known unto God" (Phil. 4:6).

If I were going to buy a house, I'd: Pray about it. Sit down and see if we could budget the extra expense in. Talk it over with the family. Go to the bank and ask for a Loan (not too many of us have that much cash on hand). Pray that the loan be approved and then give God the Glory for answered prayer.

If I wanted a friend from church to bake me a homemade butter pound cake drizzled with lemon icing, I'd: Pray and ask God to touch her heart to bless me with the cake (especially if I didn't have any money), pay her for her ingredients and labor, or I'd just ask her for one. All the person could do is to say, "No; I don't have the time right now," or "I can't do it today, but I could bake you one another day."

We also have to make our request known to people when we desire something. The person could say, "All right." Your heart may desire the house or the cake, but you have to put forth an effort to obtain your blessings. You have to also put pride aside. What if she said, "No"? What would that person think of me? Would she think that I was greedy or that I didn't need the cake after all? Remember, we may not have something because we didn't ask for it or asked for it amiss.

Care About Someone

The following letter was to a *sister in the Lord* who had a spirit of Bulimia.[32] She is a dear friend of mine and I was very concerned about her welfare. I had found an article in my local newspaper concerning the disease and was urged by the Holy Spirit

[32]A habitual disturbance in eating behavior mostly affecting young women of normal weight, characterized by frequent episodes of grossly excessive food intake followed by self-induced vomiting to avert weight gain

to send it to her along with this letter. I hope that it may also help someone else troubled with this condition.

Dear Sister _____,

You are very dear to me, and I hope that what I am about to say will not disrupt our friendship. If I have missed it (the Lord's message that I was instructed to give to you), please forgive me and pray that I hear the Lord better next time. I am using "I" throughout this letter because you know it is we (God and me) who are speaking to you, and that our God is in both of us.

My concern is your weight loss. If you remember, I did ask you how you lost all that weight so fast, and you never gave me a response. No; no one in your family told me anything about your sudden weight lost You once told me, when we were in ________ (location) about how you lost weight once before and that your family did not approve. I am not going to lecture to you, but I would like to share an article I came upon along with a few scriptures. At first, I was going to send you this anonymously so you wouldn't get upset with me, but the Lord told me to do it this way (using the computer because it's faster—not impersonal). I too, am trying to lose some weight but by natural means. If "the three Ds" (diet, discipline and discipleship) doesn't work for you anymore; there are other ways.

Would you introduce the way that you are losing weight to a church group? Your body is a temple of the Holy Spirit and we know that God dwells in a *clean temple* (*I Cor. 6:19*). And, if I were a *weak* Christian, and was in the same situation of wanting to reduce; should I follow your example? If my physical body couldn't take the strain, what would you do? Would you be able to carry the responsibility of my death for following your pattern? *(Romans 14)*

It has taken me awhile in prayer to our Father before I could confront you with this letter Sister _____. I love you and your family, and I don't want anything to happen to you. Again, if I am wrong about this situation, let me know and pray for me. But, if I am right, know that I am here for you, and we can get through this together.

Sincerely,

Your Sister in Christ

Enclosure

Our physical bodies are not our own. They are on loan to us from our Father, to do His will. We have seventy-plus years' of life expectancy on earth, and I believe that our bodies were made to endure that life span. We are not supposed to abuse our bodies with overeating, or any other form of abuse (i.e. drugs, alcohol or cutting). It is our responsibility to exercise proper care in what we do to our bodies in moderation and take care of what God has given us just as much as we take care of that new automobile, home, child, or other possession that He has blessed us with. Have you noticed how very well-preserved many Christians, who are doing the will of God, actually look? They look marvelous, and so can you!

Stay Home and Rest Awhile

What happens if you are invited to a worldly affair (such as an award dinner, or a going away party), and it's on a church night? Which do you attend? Where is your priority? Well, if it is going to over-exert your body, you may have to say "No" to both engagements because you had too many other activities during that day. As stated in Robert Liardon's book, *Learning to Say NO! Without Feeling Guilty*[33], a Christian can say "No" and stay saved. It's how we say it, and for which reasons we say "no", that really matter.

Not forsaking the assembling of ourselves together, as the manner of some is; but exhorting one another: and so much the more, as ye see the day approaching (*Heb. 10:25*). This scripture speaks for itself.

If I have too many social obligations, and they're keeping me away from church, then I have to eliminate some of the social engagements and also not allow my spirit man to be exhausted either.

"Sorry Lord"

Act of Contrition

> *"Oh my God, I am heartily sorry for having offended thee. And I detest all my sins because of thy just punishment; but most of all, because I have offended Thee, my God, who art All-Good and worthy of all my love. I firmly resolve, with the help of Thy Grace, to sin no more and to avoid the near occasions of sin. Amen."*[34]

No more sin! *"Let not sin reign in your mortal bodies…" (Rom. 6:11-15).* What is sin? Sin is an offense against the laws of God. What may be seen as sin to one person may not seem to be sin to another.

---

[33] Breaking Controlling Powers; Embassy Pub.; 2005, Irvine, Ca.
[34] http://www.catholicculture.org/culture//liturgicalyear/prayers/view.cfm?id=974

How people see sin depends upon their personal beliefs and their upbringing.

A friend of mine would not go to see a *movie* at a theater, but this same person would watch the video when it came out. Movie theaters are not sinful, but they convicted him. I will not watch, nor allow my TVs to be tuned to: "Roseanne," "Married with Children," "The Simpson's," or "Bevis and Butthead," and several other shows. To me, viewing them would be a sin and below my standards. Let's not do anything to offend our Father. *"But if you have doubts about whether or not you should eat something, you are sinning if you go ahead and do it. For you are not following your convictions. If you do anything you believe is not right, you are sinning" (Rom. 14:23 LB).*

Patience

Take a look at the Bible and the distance between the pages. From the time of creation in Genesis until the destruction with the flood (Noah's time) it only took six chapters within one book for God to get fed-up with His people. Now, just look at the thickness in the number of pages, of the rest of the Old Testament. God was very patient. He promised never to destroy the earth with water again (fire, is to be the way next time *II Pet. 3:10*).

Consider the New Testament and the time that has elapsed since John's first encounter with Jesus *(John chapter 1)*, hasn't God been *very* patient? No one knows how long God will strive with mankind. The time is growing very near and isn't it better for us to be ready than to be caught with our work undone?

Perfect

"Be ye therefore perfect, even as your Father which is in heaven is perfect" (*Mat. 5:48*). Not better than our brother, not boastful, or selfish, but we are to aim for excellence. No, we are not perfect, yet we are to strive towards that which is perfect and that is: *Christ likeness* (being just like Christ in our living, working, and behavioral habits while here on earth).

Seeking the Right Thing

I've noticed that people will search for a church that may teach the Word of God but doesn't live the Word. These same people tend to seek a comfortable atmosphere that doesn't raise an eyebrow about their smoking or drinking alcohol. They yearn for a church that looks the other way if a wife is being abused by her husband, or a church where the father-figure or mother-figure doesn't devote time to their family.

When some people are instructed from God's Word about what to do, and it doesn't agree with what their flesh is comfortable with, those persons tend to seek higher ground (another church that will tell them what they want to hear). *Seek* and *do* the Word of God.

Christian Woman!

"Look! Up in the Sky; It's a Bird! It's a Plane! No, It's Christian Woman!"

Have you ever met someone who was so friendly at church, and, when you meet them in the streets, or around another setting other than church, they are totally different? Being associated with the military, I have come in contact with some Christians who have a Chameleon-like attitude. They change according to whichever setting they're in: very loving to you around other saints and very distant when around you and other people in the world.

We should be the same in our spirit man at all times and in every setting in which we are physically involved. We should portray an image of Christ and show His love to people we meet. So too, as the Word of God is the same yesterday, today, and forever; we should be also.

I Serve a Big God

I was taught in Catholic school that, out of reverence and respect, any reference to the name of God should be CAPITALIZED!

Spirits vs. Spirits

Let's consider the drinking of alcoholic beverages (beer, wine coolers [social drinking], and etc.) My husband and I were invited to a wedding rehearsal dinner where champagne was served in celebration. My husband Van was the minister for the wedding. We know what the Word says about doing everything decently and in order *(I Cor. 14:40)*. *Phil. 4:5* also states, "*Let your moderation be known unto all men. The Lord is at hand.*" And let us not forget the fourteenth chapter of Romans which tells us that we are not to lead anyone astray because of what we consider to be right or wrong. Yet, how are we to be an effective witness if we partake of the grape even a little bit? Yes, we are human, and we may know when to stop, but our example may lead someone else astray, and they may not be able to stop. So we chose not to have any champagne.

The Word says that Jesus attended a wedding and turned water into wine *(John 2:1-10)*, but does it say that He partook of the grape Himself? Jesus and Mary had to keep their wits about themselves. They couldn't take a chance and fall into temptation. Let's just believe that they didn't have any wine.

You say, "Jesus drank wine at the Last Supper." Well, so did many people throughout the scriptures, both the old and the new. Some sinned due to over-indulgence; some made bad decisions under the influence, and others were just "*merry old souls.*" Yet, when Jesus took bread and wine, blessed it, and said, "This is My body and blood;" wine took on a different significance *(Mat. 26:26-28)*.

Remember, in that day and time, people did not have soda, Kool Aid, ™ or coffee, and wine was a part of their diet. They were raised to drink wine for nourishment, and I do believe that there was innocence to the fermentation process. I guess what I am finally saying concerning this matter is that a person should let the Holy

Spirit lead them. *"In all thy ways acknowledge Him, and He shall direct thy paths"* (*Prov. 3:6*). And remember what our mission on this earth is: to stay saved and help someone else receive salvation. *"Let not sin therefore reign in your mortal body, that ye should obey it in the lusts thereof"* (*Rom. 6:12*).

"Homo vs. Hetero?" - No Question

Is it a wonder that you don't see two dogs of the same sex trying to *get it on* together, or any animal trying to have sex with their same sex? God did not intend for same sexes to come together in an unnatural relationship. The intercourse between two males or two females will never reproduce an offspring. Then why does man, who is higher than the animals, become gender confused with homosexuality and heterosexuality.

Man, who has intelligence that is superior to the animal species, has gender-disorder problems. Man, the same creature that God made a little lower than the angels *(Ps. 8:4-5)* has a problem. God didn't put confusion of gender in this world, so who did? God knew what He created when He created man and woman: *"So God created man in his own image, in the image of God created he him; male and female created he them"* (*Gen. 1:27*). God is not confused and neither should man be.

More About Sin

Whether original sin, mortal sin, venial sin, or near-occasion of sin; it's *all* sin. Sin has no classification or degree according to the Bible. It is a perpetration (a crime committed) against any law of God. When we sin, we fall from God's graces. But there is hope and forgiveness in the confession of our sins, and repentance for those sins. It's not about just saying we're sorry for the moment, and then committing that same sin over and over again, but being whole-heartily sorry and then trying, with the help of God, *not* to commit that sin again.

Fixed Income

"I can't pay my tithes because I'm living on a fixed income." This is a statement that should not be spoken by any Christian who believes in the power of Almighty God. First of all, we *can* do *all* things through Christ *(Phil. 4:13)*. The word "can't" is a word, which should *not* be in our vocabulary. Secondly, there are many Christian financial advisors available, who will help you manage your money today, so you will not have future worries. We are living in a time where we must depend on God and the resources <u>He</u> has given us.

Sure we have to use the word <u>not</u> sometimes, but I have curtailed my use of the word <u>cannot</u>. There may be some things I *won't* do or *might not* do, but I ***can do*** anything I set my mind to by the grace of God.

Superstition

Ladies, your purse being placed on the floor will not make you *poor*. You can put it down—but don't leave it unattended—and prosper. Remember, every one in church isn't saved or honest.

Tithes

You are attending a church and feeding (learning about God's Word) quite well. You are also growing in God's grace. If you have missed service a couple of times, the pastor sees to it that someone comes to see about you or to see if you are ill. When you die would the pastor and church body, where you now attend, be there to comfort your loved ones who have been left behind? Then why would you take 10% of what you earn and give it to someone and somewhere other than where you are being nurtured? It seems that this sanctuary, where you now attend, is investing something in you, so why shouldn't that place receive the best of and from you?

That 10% *belongs* to the Lord and is supposed to go to the building up of His kingdom *(Mal. 3:8-10)*. If God's kingdom is to excel here on earth, then that need of support should also have its start here. If I gave birth to a child today, and I took responsibility for the child, wouldn't I be wrong to deprive and neglect my child by sending my money and dedicating my time to a child in another country? I'm not saying that the child in another country should not benefit from my support, but we must first tend to that for which God has given us personal responsibility. So too, should we take care of our church where we are physically and spiritually being fed. You may have a church back home where you may once *have had* an allegiance, but that was then, and this is now.

Allegiance

It has been brought to my attention how some Christians are stuck in the place (i.e., your Grand Mama's church) where they were first saved, water baptized, and filled with the precious Holy Spirit, and they are not receiving any *spiritual nourishment* from that church; they need to get out and go where they can be fed. Some people may even feel that a particular chair or pew belongs solely to them because of their money contributions. I have even heard some people say that the place where you were water baptized is the church that you joined for life and to whom you should give your faithfulness.

When we are baptized—in the name of the Father, the Son, and the Holy Spirit—*that* is to whom we pledge our lives and allegiances. Remember that Baptism is an outward sign of an inward change. The old man is gone, and we are now new creations in Christ Jesus *"Therefore if any man be in Christ, he is a new creature: old things are passed away; behold, all things are become new" (II Cor. 5:17).*

We should hold dear those memories of where we were first reinstated with Christ, yet our loyalty should travel with us as we move. Yes, we should have a home church, but that church should be located where we are currently living, where we are being spiritually fed, and where our tithes (money and time) are given.

If God places it upon your heart to give an offering (that financial gift that is given over our tithes) somewhere else, then by all means do that; but pay your allegiance (tithes) to the place where you are growing in God's Word. If that church is not where you are physically located, then, in order to receive *spiritual nourishment*, you need to get to the place where the *church that nourishes* you is located.

Stealing

A sore subject upon which I am about to speak, is directed especially towards Christians. You know there's a little statement in the front of a DVD, videotape or a CD that you either buy or rent. It's the blurb (a brief advertisement or announcement) that we all buzz past. It lets us know that *copying* the material from the original source to another source is a *felony*. It's <u>*stealing*</u>.

I used to be guilty of that crime too, especially when I'd hear a good gospel tape and didn't have enough money to own my own original. Justification always played a big role in the copying process. "It's Christian music," or "It's a blessing." Yeah, and it was stealing to dub off the original recording without permission of the owner.

Those whom God have blessed with the talent to produce their materials (music or movie) are losing their financial blessings, and, if you copied their materials, then you are the *thief*. It's not right and cannot be justified.

If there's a particular CD, video or tape that I desire, then I ask the Lord and budget my funds to acquire it. You never know, but, if you put forth the effort and let your request be made known, someone may be encouraged to bless you with your own *original* recording. No need to steal when blessings are always available.

The World Didn't Give It, and the World Can't Take It Away

I used to say, "If someone *stole* something from me, then that person may have needed the item more than I did." WRONG! I don't say that anymore. "Why?" You may ask.

When you have something that *you have taken care of*, remember that it was *God* who gave that possession to you in the first place. If He wanted others to have the same thing don't you know that *He* has the power and resources to give the same thing to those other people? Envy and stealing are sins. If you're not careful, one may lead to the other.

Scrumdidileyumschious!

God is all that, and then some. He's all that, and He made the *bag of chips*. He is *All* Mighty, *All* Powerful, *All* Merciful, *All* Loving, *All* Knowing, and so much more.

Chow Time

I once heard a Christian woman say this prayer over her food, "Lord I hope that I won't gain any weight from what I'm about to eat and all that I'm about to eat." I used to say a similar prayer, "Bless us, oh Lord, and these Thy gifts which we are about to receive from Thy bounty, through Christ our Lord; and let this food cause me no excess weight." Well, the meal was blessed, I gave thanks, and that was about it.

The Word tells us that we should watch how we take care of these human bodies. We should do all things in moderation and not be gluttonous. *"Let all things be done decently and in order" (I Cor. 14:40).* Please read *Romans 14.* Besides exercising our faith, we should also exert these bodies of ours. Even those persons who have a super metabolism, and who can eat anything, while not tipping the scales either way, should show self-control for themselves and in front of others while consuming food.

I believe that a little fat won't hurt you, if you keep it to a minimum. My grandparents lived to be in their 70s and didn't have the knowledge of which foods would harm them, except that too much *pork* could elevate their blood pressure. We should eat to live and enjoy eating in moderation.

A Secret Place?

There is no secret to what God *can* and *will* do in your life if you continually take a little time with Him. I don't have a *prayer closet,* yet my quiet place of meditation is usually the bathroom. It's no secret that when I'm in there, it's usually quiet time with me and my Lord. I can be putting on my make-up and before I know it, I'm done and I've had a great meeting with Him. Also, during this time of peace, I receive a lot of inspiration from Him that I carefully write down. I don't spend hours in that one quiet place, but the time spent is quality time.

Motivation

Some people spend money buying *motivational tapes*, pay money and take time to see a *motivational speaker*; but don't people realize that the principles, which are used in most speakers' influential speeches, come directly from the Bible?

You want outside stimuli? Read your Bible. If Job wasn't motivated, through his belief in God—in spite of all the adversity around him—then there is no such thing as outside encouragement, but there is such a thing as seen in the Bible. What about Joseph? He had to face near death at the hands of his brothers, deception, seduction (being lied on), and then was tossed into prison, yet he became a chief leader in Egypt (Please read *Genesis chapters 37 – 47*; it's a great read). Now <u>that's</u> *motivation*!

Xmas?

If Christmas is the day we celebrate as Christ's birth (Dec. 25th, according to Webster's Dictionary), then what is the abbreviation "Xmas" all about? If "X" is the mathematical symbol for the unknown, then "X"-mas must mean the celebration of the unknown.

Jesus Christ is *known* by many people to be the Son of God. He is not an unknown factor. It is our responsibility to tell everyone about Jesus. Christians—let's help everyone put Christ back into Christmas and take the "X" out. "Merry Christ – mas"!

Somebody's Watching You

I do believe that curve balls are thrown our way to see what we will do and how we, as Christians, will react to certain situations.

For instance, a person at work does you an injustice, and everyone that's standing around you knows that you should be upset. You have the right to retaliate and throw a hissy-fit, but instead of going off, you hold your peace. People wonder how you can be so cool or how come you didn't slap that person right up side their head. You were offended and had the right. Wrong! It was the power of the Holy Spirit that kept you and helped you to hold your tongue and your hands. You have just been a witness for God and His kingdom. Wow! You may even have been the cause of someone giving his or her life to Jesus by your example. "You go boy (girl)!"

Making the Difference

You never know when it's your prayer that makes the difference in someone's life. Have you ever thought that your prayer was not necessary for someone else to make it through?

You probably knew that other people were praying for the same thing so why should God bother with your little prayer? You never know. Your one little request may be the one that God is waiting to hear. So don't count yourself short. Your prayers *do* count.

Heard It Through the Grapevine

Watch that the *grapevine*[35] doesn't turn into the *gossipvine* at your workplace.

The grapevine is an important asset in the workplace. A lot of times we find out about promotions, opportunities, advancements, gatherings, incentives, and etc. all through the grapevine. The *gossip vine* discusses other people, and their private or personal business, and often has the "facts" misconstrued or just plain wrong. The *gossip vine* is usually cruel and unfeeling. The *gossip vine* tears down; it doesn't build up. Don't be a part of confusion in your workplace.

Let's Give Jesus A Hand

Recognize what God has done for you in your life and be thankful. Have you ever been driving along and realized that the request you asked God for last month has already been fulfilled? For example: you used to have asthma, and you realize that you haven't had to use your inhaler in weeks. When that happens, take that moment to *thank* Him for His goodness. It doesn't have to be an elaborate prayer in front of a group of people. He appreciates hearing from us at anytime.

---

[35]a person-to-person method of spreading rumors, gossip, information, etc., by informal or unofficial conversation, letter writing, or the like.

"Joy" Fruit of the Spirit (Gal. 5:22)

Mr. Webster defines *Joy* as gladness, exhilaration of spirits, to rejoice; to exalt.

Joy is an emotion, a feeling, and an exhilaration of oneself and it's a happy face. It's an ice cream cone on a hot summer's day. Joy is a baby's smile. It's your husband's love. It's good news. Joy is sunshine. It's a walk at night after a summer rain. Joy is remembering the *good* in the good old days. Joy is a thank you. Joy is Jesus Christ.

Joy is part of the fruit of God's spirit. An orange has sections. It's one piece of fruit, yet it contains many sections. So, too, is the fruit of the Holy Spirit. There is one fruit with nine different attributes (seeds or sections). You can't buy an orange and not get all of the seeds with it. Even navel oranges have very tiny seeds, and those seeds are needed to grow more oranges.

If you desire the fruit of God's Spirit (and you *should* want His Spirit), then take all of the seeds that come from the fruit. If you don't have any of the seeds (gifts), pray for them and receive them. It's that easy. And you won't want to spit out those seeds.

Welfare

Welfare – financial or other assistance to an individual or family from a city, state, or national government.

There is no shame in being on welfare. The shame comes when people, both men and women, stay on the system with no signs of coming off.

I was once on welfare when my son was born. I went to nursing school and became a Licensed Practical Nurse (LPN), went to two years of college before I wrote the Department of Welfare and thanked them for their support during that time of need. I didn't abuse the system but used it to my advantage. The system was designed to help you help yourself, and it was *not* intended to be a *permanent crutch* for your lifestyle.

Welfare should not be an inherited condition either. Family members should try to encourage the next generation to stay away from *public assistance* instead of being a *slave* to it. Some friends of mine, with whom I grew up, had mothers, who were on welfare, yet those children have married or remained single, and they've become successful in the workforce. They stopped the cycle of dependence. You too can be an over comer. The choice is yours. It's up to you to make the right decisions.

Taking Advantage

Have you ever been invited to a sit-down dinner at someone's home just to find out that you were invited with the intention that you would purchase the *cookware*, which was to be used to make the dinner? Or have you been invited to someone's house and received a free *this or that* just for coming over to hear someone attempt to tell you about the product they need to sell to you in order to make themselves some money? Some people flock to these types of invitations, knowing they're not going to purchase anything, but they only come to get the freebies.

It's not right to do this, just as it's not right for Christians to file for bankruptcy because they've lost control of their finances or made a bad decision (without the aid of the Holy Spirit). If we follow God's directions, then there is no failure in what we can do.

I've spoken with some other people who have *taken advantage* of a system (welfare) as an easy way out of a situation, and those persons have not had any success in their lives.

It's up to each individual to take care of how they handle all of the freebies that are handed out in life. How would you feel if you were selling a product and the only reason people showed up was just to get the free stuff and nothing more? You would probably be hurt by their inconsiderate behavior.

No Fear

You may often see the words "No Fear" on articles of clothing and various signs. In reality, people today have no fear. They have no fear of parents, no fear of consequences, no fear of authority, and no fear of *God.* As they step out into the world today, spiritually unarmed, many children are expressing this same no fear attitude. Parents, encourage your children to wear their whole armor and leave the "No-Fear" gear to the world.

Eat, Drink and Be Merry?

"*Eat, Drink And Be Grouchy.*" "I like that," said one department store customer to the other as she viewed some writing on a *sleep shirt.* She liked the saying that this particular cartoonist drew on her greeting cards and articles of clothing. Isn't it sad that some older, more mature people view our world and society with such a grim outlook?

A little while later that same day, another lady bought the same type of *sleep shirt.* She was going to wear the shirt to her daughter's sleepover at school, which consisted of four- and five-year-olds accompanied by their mothers. What a fashion statement. What a negative example she was setting for the little ones at the sleepover. Sometimes it's not just what we say, but what we wear that makes a difference. What are you saying?

It seems that long ago there was a similar saying with a negative outlook, "Eat, Drink and Be Merry, For Tomorrow We

Die." God's Word states, *"Let us eat and drink; for tomorrow we shall die" (Isaiah 22: 13 , I Cor. 15:32 and Ecc. 8:15).* The Word says that we should watch what we say and do (blessings and cursing come from the same tongue (*Deut. 30:19)*, because we will eventually have that which we speak into existence (*Prov. 18:21* and *Mk. 11:23).* Ready? Set? Grab your Bibles!

I Don't Wanna Lord

When God commands us to do a certain thing, we don't always have to like what we're about to do. God knows the whole plan that He has given us. We should have a pleasant attitude when we undertake any task given by the Father. The assignment may not be a desire of our heart, but it's God's desire that the task be completed and accomplished by whomever He chooses for the task.

As we joyfully obey God, He grants us the desires of our heart. *"Delight thyself also in the LORD: and he shall give thee the desires of thine heart"* (*Ps. 37:4*). For example, God wants you to send someone a thank you note, but you don't *feel* that the person deserves a thank you. They did a favor which you consider was expected of them. You *feel* that verbal thanks are enough. Well, that note, which the Lord said for you to send, may be the catalyst that was needed to bring that person closer to Christ and their personal salvation. We don't always know, but God does.

Open Sez-A-Me

Have you ever heard the saying, "When God closes a door, He opens a window?" The saying *should* be, "When we close the door, God opens a window."

God does not give us blessings and then take them away from us when we keep Him first in our lives. It is *we* who allow the enemy to come in and take what God has given to us. God bestows blessings upon us, and it is up to us to keep and use the blessings He gives.

God's Got a Super Highway

If you think the Internet is something, then tap into the *power of prayer with God*, and get the expected and the unexpected.

Sore Tootsies

One Wednesday evening, my pastor had given a thought-provoking message. I pulled him aside after service to let him know that I was "going home to *soak my feet* because the Word of God just tap-danced all across my toes." That's what happens when you're in tune with the spirit of God. Conviction or recognition occurs when you hear a message that God directs especially towards you. When you realize that God is speaking directly to you, just listen, hear, and obey.

Who's On First?

God	**Me**	**Family**	**Work**
First	***Second***	***Third***	***Fourth***

God will lead and guide you through the affairs of your life. *You* have to take care of your health and see about your needs (not wants) before you can take care of anyone else. This also means that you don't go to the poor farm trying to go overboard buying yourself things you can't afford. Your *family* will always be there for you. And you need to *work* and get along with your co-workers in order to reap the salary that God has supplied you through your position at work. It's the order of things that brings success to your life. These four important elements should be in everyone's life.

How would you handle the following situation? One evening, you are scheduled to go to your child's music recital. You are also expected to attend a going-away party for a co-worker at the office, and, on the same night, there is a revival at church—all events are scheduled to start at 7:00 p.m. Tough situation? Well, there are different ways to view these events. Let me tell you how I would prioritize the situation.

My child, who is a gift from God, needs my support in all that he/she attempts to do. Either my husband and/or I would be there for them. Usually, the revival will run more than one night. I would let my pastor know that I wouldn't be able to make it on that night, but, Lord willing (and He is), I would try to make it on another night. My co-workers, especially the one leaving, should be given an explanation of why I won't be able to stay at the party long. If it has been placed upon my heart to give the person leaving a gift, then I would do so, along with my apology.

At this time, let me mention that our children's activities can also pull us away from other duties that we have in our lives. I have seen some parents be slaves to their children's ambitions and neglect their own personal duties. There *is* a happy medium, and, during family discussion times, compromises can be made for all concerned. Also, don't try to do everything in one night because you do need to get some rest too.

Who or What Are You a Slave To?

What is a ***slave***? A slave is a person who is the property of, and subject to another; a bondservant, a person entirely under the domination of some influence or person. Slaves always have something or someone controlling their lives.

What are some things that a person can be a slave to? Let's take a look:

Automobiles – A car will put you into debt if you try to get the fastest, the most expensive, or the most popular version instead of something that is affordable or economical (and I'm also talking about those cars that have a stereo system that's worth more than the car itself). A motor vehicle may keep you away from church and family while it gets your attention cleaning, polishing, tweaking, and updating it's every physical and mechanical composition, if you allow it to.

Children – Yes, your children can make you their slave in more ways than one. Baseball games, soccer, music lessons, ballet, basketball, drama, and the list goes on and on. Now, there's nothing wrong with desiring that your children have things better than you did, but do let it be the decision of the child. Also for those of you who are divorced or separated parents, don't try to do everything that you can to be the child's *friend* by trying to fill the gap of the other missing parent. If we allow them to, children can manipulate us. It's okay to *befriend* our children, but we must remember that we are the parents and we have a commission to train our children in the way that they should go.

Drugs – Alcohol, cigarettes, tranquilizers, painkillers, sedatives, hashish, marijuana, codeine, TCP, smack, crack, and the list goes on. Such drugs have caused numerous families grief, separation, financial burdens, and even death. What started out as *just an experiment*, at one time, may have turned into a dependency problem after prolonged use.

Food – Eating when you're not hungry. Consuming too much or the wrong types of foods will enslave you to other medical ailments such as obesity, heart trouble, diabetes, high blood pressure, bulimia, and possibly even death.

Time Management – When you waste precious time that you cannot retrieve; then you are subject to time deprivation (the absence, loss, or withholding of something needed). Always being late for appointments is oppressive. Not meeting deadlines at work can also be burdensome and can cause friction in the workplace or even loss of employment.

TV – Television has become a form of babysitting and a tool to lure people away from improving their minds by reading, participating in outdoor activities, or challenging their minds. This visual suppression also includes playing video games, watching DVDs, and yes, even being on the Internet for too long will affect your body, your mind, and your time management. And guys, just how many sports channels do you really need to put a wedge between you and your loved ones?

Shopping – Ladies (and some men), let's not be under the dominion of a charge card, a one-day-sale, or the temptation of buying something that we don't need or can't afford.

There are other influences that can put us into bondage if we allow them to. The main solution to avoiding *slavery* is to concentrate on *servitude*. Serving God and other people helps us towards healthier relationships *(Psalms 84:10)*.

This writer would rather be a *servant (a* person in the service of another) of the *most high God* and follow in the footsteps of biblical persons such as Paul and Silas *(Acts 16:17)* or Shadrach,

Meshach, and Abednego (*Dan 3:26)*, than to be a slave to someone or something that may be harmful to my life and my relationship with God. Think about it, even politicians are called public servants.

Being Humble, Not Humiliated

We can have a sweet cool spirit, and a calm disposition without appearing defeated. God does not want us to be slaves to anyone, not even Him. There is a difference between a servant and a slave.

A *servant* is glad to do almost anything for his master (even unto death). He is accustomed to doing well for his employer, and it brings the servant pleasure to please him. A servant usually *chooses* to obey.

A *slave*, however, is bound or forced to serve. Usually, he is in chains and is forced to do whatever his master says. If he had a choice, he would be somewhere else and doing something else. It does not give the slave joy to serve. A slave is *made* to obey.

Look at Gehazi who served under Elisha (*II Kings 4:12 - 27; 5:20-27)* or the servant with the five *talents* in the New Testament (*Mat. 25:20-21)*. Even the Prodigal Son realized that the servants in his father's house were living better than he was (*Luke 15:17)*.

The word *slave* is used once in the scriptures *(Jer. 2:14)* and the word *slaves* is also used only once (*Rev. 18:13)*. Don't you know that I would rather be a **servant** of the Most High God than a **slave** to anything?

Listen To What You Hear

Have you had the opportunity to sit somewhere that is quiet, and then taken the time to listen to the birds sing? Have you ever listened to the different sounds outside? Are we able to hear those audible remembrances which we often take for granted? Can we listen to people quietly talking in their gardens, children laughing while they play, and a lawn mower cutting grass way off in the distance, or music playing softly in the background and be appreciative of God's symphony? It's music to one's ears.

During these peaceful times of being still and listening, I can reminisce about the good times when I was younger. It reminds me of what I was doing when I heard those same sounds years ago such as going roller skating, having picnics in the park, or going to a friend's house for a party. It's a very precious feeling that I get when I think about these experiences. It's also during those quiet times that I can hear the voice of God without difficulty.

We Have To Realize God

Once we learn what God has for us and what his purpose is in our lives, then we will be prosperous, victorious, and walk in a renewed lifestyle.

Dueling Paper Mates™

"The pen is mightier than the sword," is a famous quote that was penned by Edward Bulwer-Lytton. I don't believe that Mr. Bulwer-Lytton was referring to the Word of God (the Bible) when he spoke about the sword, but, what he may have meant is that you don't have to get violent and retaliate if a situation is not right.

We Christians *should* voice our opinion, especially when our human rights are violated. If there is a movie that comes to our town, we have the choice to voice our concerns. First, we should not go to see that particular movie; and second, in some places, we can let the theater owner know that we don't appreciate that type of movie to be shown in our town. This works better in smaller communities. Next, we can write the movie company and express our concerns and get others to write as well. Sure, it takes time to write, but, if we want to see change, we must *take the time* to make a difference.

Live and Let Live

Why do some people use the expression, "I love you to death?" Do we wish that person evil or harm? Remember, our tongue has the power of life and death, or blessings and cursing. If we must love someone, let's love them to life.

Fear vs. Faith

And he said unto them, Why are ye so fearful? How is it that ye have no faith (*Mark 4:40*)*?*

Once upon a time, I was very afraid of bees. When one would come anywhere near me, I would run. No, I was not allergic to their sting, but I had nightmares about them attacking me. And when I heard about the "killer bees," I was ready to go to the other side of the earth to be away from them. I had *it* bad.

During one nightmare, I finally prayed to God and actually called out to Him in my sleep. There was a giant bee that was coming directly at my jugular vein (the large vein in your neck). The bee was going to stab me with its giant stinger. God woke me up with the scripture of *Mark 4:40*. Mind you, I was not very familiar with my Bible, so, when I read the passage, I was surprised that it was about being afraid just as I had been. Since that day, I have had *no* fear of a bee, and I have never been stung. I don't play with bees, yet I respect their territory; nevertheless, if one comes across my path, I won't cross the street to avoid them.

Shower Full-O-Blessings

When your desire *("Delight thyself also in the Lord: and he shall give thee the desires of thine heart" Ps. 37:4)* lines up with God's will (His divine order), then you will receive a multitude of blessings.

Don't Wanna Go

It's not good when some folks *steal* other people's *joy* by gossiping, being deceitful, being two-faced, by lying, or by being hypocritical. These mean-spirited persons take the excitement and desire out of loving people who used to go to church to hear the Word of God and fellowship with others. And just because of what someone did or said, the person who used to go stops going to church. I've seen some new believers (those persons who have come to know God for the first time), and some seasoned saints (those who have attended church for years) leave a church due to hurtful backbiting and hypocrisy.

People shouldn't stay at home and say that they'll get *it* (the Word—God's message) from reading *their* Bible or listening to a preacher on TV. Sometimes God speaks to us through other people (especially children), and His wisdom and knowledge is also shared through an earthly shepherd (Pastor) under whose instruction He desires us to be.

Heavenly Brownie Points

You don't want to be sorry that you haven't made more spiritual deposits into your heavenly bank account. A heavenly deposit is defined as what we do on this earth now, which will eventually count later when we reach our heavenly home *(Mat. 25:21)*.

Why should we give up a chance to bless someone and be blessed when we continually use statements like:

Should have: "I should have asked the new neighbor in for a cup of coffee and a chat"

Would have: "If they dressed better, I would have invited them to church"

Could have: "If I knew they were really hungry, I could have bought them some groceries"

By doing good things in this life, we will be blessed *now* and also *later* *(Mat. 6:3-4 and Lk. 6:35-38)*. It also wouldn't hurt us to give more compliments to each other. God prompts us now and then to let someone know that they're doing a good job, that they look nice today, or that we really appreciated them.

How are your deposits coming? Are you making your deposits now, so you won't regret your retirement plan later?

Believe and Receive

You may ask, "If God is able, then why doesn't He…?"

"Why doesn't He *heal* me?"

"Why doesn't He *use me* for His service?"

"Why doesn't He prove *this* or *that* to me?"

Well, first of all, God is sovereign (having supreme rank, power, or authority). He doesn't have to *prove* anything. Sometimes He does, but that's up to Him. He is Elohim (the Creator). He is El Shaddai (the all-sufficient one). He is God.

Secondly, the reason why God may not show Himself to you is because of your unbelief in *this* or *that* situation. Or it may be because of a lack of faith. Yes, I too sometimes have to build up my faith level in a particular area. I'm striving to achieve the level that Brother Smith Wigglesworth had. Through the power and anointing of God, he once resurrected a woman from the dead. He slammed her against a wall and spoke life back into her body. (Was that the first method of CPR[36]—the Holy Ghost way?)

Yes, our faith has to be built up, and we do this by praying to our Father and asking for an extra dose of the *Gift of Faith*. Then, while awaiting the manifestation of the gift of faith, we must ***believe*** that we have received it. In other words: *trust*, *believe*, *and receive.*

[36] Cardiopulmonary Resuscitation - an emergency procedure consisting of external cardiac massage and artificial respiration.

Praising <u>God</u> or Praising god?

Material possessions, which you acquire during your lifetime, can be a touchy subject to talk about, but let me attempt to take a stab at it. We are not to treat *things*, with which we have been blessed, as if they were our *gods*.

We clean our cars on Sunday instead of going to worship God, who bestowed the blessing of the automobile upon us in the first place, so we could travel better.

Our children can be idols too. Sometimes, we give them everything they desire. We don't consider how our actions will affect their future growth toward adulthood. We must teach them that people don't always get what they want and they must work for what they want.

If we allow them to be, our knickknacks (small ornamental articles; a trinket), which we put on display to collect dust, can be our gods. If one is accidentally broken, we may be led to swear, or to say something bad about the person who had the misfortune of damaging our delicate object. It was God who blessed us with the financial means to pay for these things anyhow.

God *gave* them, or should I say, He *entrusted* these possessions to us. He is waiting to see how we handle these gifts. Should He give us more? Did we thank Him for what He has already given us? Let's praise God from whom all blessings flow.

Can I Borrow…?

If God has blesses us with a particular thing, shouldn't we ensure that the possession is treated as if it belonged to God (which originally it did), especially if we *loan* or entrust it to someone else? If I allow my daughter to watch your children, I expect her to be returned to me unharmed and financially rewarded for her services. If I were to loan you my lawnmower, I would expect to get it back in the same condition (or even better) as when you borrowed it. Treat every item as if you were returning it to Jesus.

On the subject of *loaning* people money and/or things: guard yourself from the possibility of sin. If you're not strong enough to stand a loss if, or when, a person doesn't repay you, then *don't loan* that particular thing to anyone. If it is money you are loaning and the person doesn't pay you back, will it affect your relationship with the person or your relationship with God? If you have doubt about a repayment, you should be willing to be in a position to *give* that thing to the person instead of just *loaning* it to them.

We shouldn't set ourselves up for a fall or sin. Be generous, yet be wise as a serpent and harmless as a dove *(Mat. 10:16)*. Know the person with whom you're dealing and seek God's guidance concerning *loaning* vs. *giving*.

Now I Really Know Him

When I attended elementary school, God instilled in my fellow classmates and me a sense of how to do things on cue while we concentrated on other things.

Let me explain. During church services, we were programmed to know when the proper time came to sit, stand or kneel, especially when we would hear certain words spoken in another language. I'm not being sacrilegious, but think about it. I was brought up in a church that ministered in Latin (a language I knew little about), and, although I was present physically, I was miles away in my mind. The times that I can recall hearing and understanding what was being taught were only during the sermons of Christmas, Easter, and Lent.

The experience *did* teach me discipline. I was instructed in religious truths each day because catechism[37] was part of the curriculum. The Word of God touched my life early, beginning in the first grade.

This man Jesus, whom I was drilled on and taught about daily, I did *not* know. I knew *of* Him, but oh! how sweet it is to really know our Savior. We are privileged to be able to learn from the Bible how we should live and conduct our lives in order to enjoy

---

[37]an elementary book containing a summary of the principles of the Christian religion, esp. as maintained by a particular church, in the form of questions and answers.

the many things which God has for us in this world and in the world to come.

Perfect Forty

My daughter Tonya once asked me, "Is the number forty God's perfect number?" She had remembered some instances in the Bible where the number forty had appeared:

Jesus wandered in the desert for forty days, and it was there that He was tempted by the devil (*Lk. 4:2*).

Moses was up on Mt. Sinai for forty day and nights (*Deut. 9:9, 10:10*).

After Noah built the great ark, it rained upon the earth for forty days and nights (*Gen. 7:4*).

The children of Israel wandered in the desert for forty years and there they were sustained by Manna from heaven (*Ex. 16:35*).

Moses sent twelve spies into Canaan, and they returned with their reports after forty days (*Num. 13:25*).

David ruled as King for forty years (*I Kings 2:11*).

After the resurrection, Jesus dwelt among His Apostles some forty days (*Acts. 1:3*).

There are numerous other accounts where forty was a primary number in God's Word, and we know that anything God has put His divine hand to is perfect.

Spiritual Boxing Gloves

The devil will temp you when and where you least expect him to tempt you. He will tempt you in an area in your life where you are the weakest.

I was once vulnerable when it came to cigarettes. Smelling them used to give me the desire to have one. There's no temptation there any more. Once it was a *fear of bees*. Now there's no seduction in that area either. Another time, I made up justification for taking *little things* for myself from the workplace (i.e., pens, paperclips, rubber bands, or other small office supplies). A little enticing, yet I had to remind myself, "Is a paper clip worth my going to hell, and burning forever, and being separated from God?" Hockey sticks, **No!**

Now I pray to God for His divine strength to rebuke the enemy when he tries to worry me about some danger happening to one of my family members. Sometimes I would envision or dream of something happening to my son, who was away in the military; or to my daughter, who was a growing teenager; or to my husband, who traveled a lot. When I would sense the devil trying to defeat my spiritual strength in any of these areas, I would pray, rebuke the devil, and then give praise to God for His love and protection.

"What if…?" I don't use the statement or think on those things that are not of Him. God is the one who is the controller, and He knows just what we can bear. He has a plan and a purpose for everything in our lives, and His will shall be done. The devil cannot take advantage of me unless I allow him to. I'm not taking any sucker punches anymore.

Lenten and New Years Resolutions

Why should we excessively examine our consciences to do good things at one or two particular times of the year? Why give up candy, meat, smoking, movies, overeating, lack of exercise, lying and etc., for a couple of weeks in atonement, and then go right back to doing the same thing afterwards, especially if that thing is not good for you?

The time frame that I am referring to is called Lent. It's the time that is designated seven weeks before Easter (Christ's resurrection). The Lenten season has been appointed by some folks as a time to *fast* from specific sins like gluttony, slothfulness, laziness, or doing and enjoying things, which are not good for the human body such as smoking, drinking alcoholic beverages, and etc. Where in the Bible is the season of Lent specified? *Prayer* and *fasting* are two ways that we may atone for our sins, yet, during Lent and on the first of January (New Year's resolution time), people promise God not to commit a particular offense again *for awhile*, and then they expect God to turn His head until they get that particular sin out of their system.

I've overheard people ask one another, "What are you giving up for Lent?" In order to get a sense of fulfillment, they offer to give up candy or another favorite food until Easter Sunday rolls around.

The definition for *atonement* (reconciliation of God and man) is to be sorry for our sins. It's the act of making a sacrifice to God by denying oneself. To do an act of atonement, just because everyone else does it, will not make it a sacrifice to God.

Mardi Gras is another date for discussion. This is a time set aside to do all the *sinning* one can do before the season of Lent begins. God help and have mercy on those persons who might *die* during a Mardi Gras celebration, and who may be doing some immoral act. If they have not asked forgiveness of any sin they may have committed, where would they open their eyes upon their death? Also, what about AIDS and other sexually-transmitted diseases and the perversion that takes place during this so-called celebration? There also have been reports that people have been robbed, maimed and taken advantage of, during this festival time. No, I have never participated in a Mardi Gras, but I do believe that consequences do happen according to what God's Word has to say (*II Tim. 3:1-7*).

Yes, I once caught myself sacrificing something for God during the Lenten season, yet I thank God that I don't have to wait until a particular time of the year to get close to our Lord and neither do you.

Lookin' Them Straight In the Eye

Whenever you talk with a person, how do you look at them? We should look a person directly in the eye—not with a threatening gaze, but with a humble, loving, and attentive look.

We should stop looking down when speaking with people and look them directly in the eye as they do us. As we relate to others whatever it is that we need to say, we should have the confidence of knowing that we have the Holy Spirit within us. We should not be intimidated, afraid or ashamed.

Reach Out and Touch

I cannot understand how some people can be part of a religious sect, which expects that person to denounce their relationships with their blood relatives if they are not a part of the organization too. Just because this denomination doesn't celebrate birthdays and holidays, don't allow a group of outsiders turn you away from your own family. Even if your family members aren't saved, how will you tell them or show them about the joy you receive from serving Jesus if you don't communicate with them? How can you show them a better way of life and happiness without personal contact? If our relatives have intentions of doing us harm, God will tell us when it's time to separate ourselves from them; in the meantime, let's stay together!

God Parenting

My family was visiting some people one time, and the mother and daughter were upset that they did not hear from or receive anything from the daughter's **godmother** at Christmastime. The godmother, for some reason, hadn't called, either.

I thought the obligation of a godparent was to assist the parents with the spiritual upbringing of the godchild. If something was to happen to the parent, and there was no other next-of-kin, then the godparent would care for both the physical and spiritual welfare of the child. I never heard the baptizer of a child *ever* mention that godparents *had* to bestow gifts. Oh, by the way, where is it recorded in the Bible to have godparents anyway? I believe people have gotten the role of godparents confused with the fairy godmother in *Cinderella.* If it's placed upon your heart to do so, there's nothing wrong with sending the godchild something, but it shouldn't be expected.

My husband and I are godparents of two children, and we are committed to their *spiritual* well-being. When someone asks you to be their child's godparent, don't accept more children to your care than you can be accountable for. Don't take on more than it is humanly possible for you to manage.

Hearing God Pt 2

We should never think that we are the only ones that God speaks to or operates through. I am blessed to hear what God has to say when He speaks through others. I go to church anticipating a Word from God. I also realize that I must have my *gift of the Discerning of Spirits* fine-tuned. There may be some *gristle* (i.e., something told to you that is contrary to the Word of God) in that portion of *meat (*the interpretation of God's Word by another person) which we receive. Remember, we should eat the meat and spit out the gristle. Don't allow people to confuse you. If you find it necessary to chew and chew (ponder or analyze the words from others), then get a stick of chewing gum and chew on that.

If what someone says is questionable, read God's Word for yourself, even if you have to get an easier translation, and discuss with your Pastor what you've heard. God will give you the understanding to live righteously and not be deceived.

Listen My Children

There may be speakers (prophets, evangelists, or teachers) in your own church, yet that church wants to have a guest speaker come in from far away. The congregation would rather hear from Elder Joe Blow of Far Away, than from Sister Sookie of the local church. Why is that? Both persons are hearing from God, aren't they? Is it because a prophet is not accepted in his/her own place? *(Lk. 4:24)*

It's almost the same as it was during the reign of Saul in the Old Testament. The people wanted a king, not just a heavenly king, but also an earthly king *(I Sam. 11)*. They got what they wanted and went from the frying pan into the fire. Sometimes we have to watch what we ask for.

It's all right to desire someone else from somewhere else to give us a Word from God, but we should watch our selection of a guest speaker. We want to hear what God has to say and not just because of the person from *whom* we choose to hear the message.

First Things First

Since the phrase, "In the name of Jesus" is the key which brings us before the seat and ears of God, then why don't we open our prayers to our Heavenly Father by using Jesus' name at the beginning of our prayers?

I'm not saying that, if we close our prayers with "In Jesus' name" God does not listen to our requests, but doesn't it make sense to use the key *before* we try to come through the door?

Are Your Antennas Up For God's Call?

Do you hear the voice of God and act upon what you hear? Is what you hear coming from the voice of God? If so, then go ahead and do what you're told with expectations of rewards from God. Nothing beats a *failure* than a *try*.

The Church Is a Business

Don't get offended and out of sorts over this topic. Allow me to explain and give you an enlightened understanding.

The primary business of a church is to *win souls* for Christ and the Kingdom of God. There are steps the church has to complete, on a regular basis, in order for it to run according to God's will.

1. The church structure and working body has to function.

   a) Bills have to be paid, utilities, mortgage, salaries, food, travel expenses (and don't just look at the pastor as being the only person to travel. Don't we, as a church body, go on trips? Don't we eat at different functions?), equipment, office supplies, books, and the list goes on. All of these bills must be met.

2) The needs of the congregation must be met.

   a) Visitations – geared to console a person's mind, soul, and physical being.

      1) Seeing those who are first-time visitors in the church.

      2) Visiting and ministering to those who are in the hospital.

      3) Care, cell, or small group leaders attend to the needs of the people on a smaller scale.

      4) Consoling those who have lost a loved one through death.

      5) Marital or Psychological Counseling.

b) Financial Needs – If a bill needs to be paid, and you have tried to "Rob Peter to pay Paul" (making sure that Peter *did* go to work to earn the money), yet you just can't seem to make the payment this month, the church is there to *assist* you. There is also some money set aside monthly for those who are transients or for the homeless. We trust God that the person in need will be able to pay their debts the next month and will have enough money left over to bless someone else after their tithes have been paid.

The church must continue to grow, and pastors are placed within each congregation to see that the needs are met, and God's will is being done. The pastor of the church cannot do everything himself, and he/she needs other help, besides that of the Holy Spirit, and that's where the staff comes into play. And yes, the staff members could volunteer their time, but for a business to operate properly, you need to have people working in their field of expertise and doing what they are *being paid* to do (after all, the staff members have families, bills, and other obligations just as the church does).

If I go to a grocery store, I expect to find a cashier at the register to add up my groceries and to tell me how much I owe. If I have to wait on someone to *volunteer*, and hope someone will be there when I choose the time to do my shopping, then I may be waiting there all day.

Do you see why the church has to be run as a business? If it's not run in a business-like manner, then there is confusion, and things cannot be accomplished according to God's will. Everyone has a part to play to make a business run smoothly, and that includes the church.

Psalm 68:11

"The Lord gave the Word: great was the company of those that publish it"

To Be Continued, Again and Again:

"Well devil, this part is done <u>again</u>. I've done it, and to God be ***<u>ALL</u>*** the Glory. Until the next volume, thank you Jesus for your gift! Amen."

For engagements or book signings, please contact

McCloud & Associates Public Relations Agency

St Petersburg, Fl

(727) 385-0691

Ms. "V" (Victoria Thomas Poller) – The 'Dear Abby' of the Christian circuit. She has a target audience that includes everyone. Her main objective is to answer questions and give advice from a Christian perspective, to all nationalities. If you're male, female, young, or more mature - Ms. "V" will touch subjects that may not come across the pulpit. You may have had the subject matter on your mind, yet she will give a reply that is Bible based and down to earth (scripture and verses included).

Don't stay away from a church, congregation or God because of previous hurts or misunderstandings. God loves you. Let her prove it.

Victoria Thomas Poller (Ms. "V") was born in Philadelphia, Penna. She's married to, Levan. They have been united in marriage for over 30 years and are the parents of Robert (age 32) and Tonya (age 26). She followed her husband in his USAF military career for over 24 years. Her other accomplishments include publishing a Christian Business Directory from 2004 – 2007; volunteering for the City of Clovis, NM; teaching women's groups and speaking engagements in the US and Europe. Besides writing non-fiction motivational books, she has written numerous grant proposals for 501C3 organizations. Check her website for the latest release or request one of her other books from your local book store.

Victoria (Ms. "V") posts blogs on her web site and other social network pages, and welcomes your comments: www.victoriapoller.com. Come by and take a look.

www.ingramcontent.com/pod-product-compliance
Ingram Content Group UK Ltd.
Pitfield, Milton Keynes, MK11 3LW, UK
UKHW020129250726
13967UKWH00002B/553